Rise up, People!

You must save America!

Also by
Eugene (E.J.) Schwarz

His Word, Our Guide;
Biblical Origins of the Christian Church

MegaMyths of Politics, Economics, and Religion

The Bible, God, Science and History

Rise up, People!

You must save America!

By

E. J. Schwarz

Rise up, People!
You must save America!

All Rights Reserved © 2018 by E. J. Schwarz

No part of this book may be reproduced or transmitted in any form or by any means, graphic, electronic, or mechanical, including photocopying, recording, taping, or by any information storage retrieval system, without written permission of the publisher.

ISBN: 978-1727640830

For permissions, email or text:
        EJ.Schwarz@outlook.com
        (719) 650-7105

Printed in the United States of America

Available on Amazon.com
        amazon.com

Dedication

In loving memory of Fr. Marian Switka, one of 816 survivors of Dachau concentration camp out of 2800 Catholic priests imprisoned there. More than 7,000 others had been killed earlier in World War II. The remaining 2000 were starved and worked to death in Dachau.

Fr. Marian, Fr. Mitchell Gawron, and Fr. Michael Glogowski, were assigned to the same work detail. Mitch became ill and could barely walk. Fearing that he would be shot, Marian and Mike carried him on their arms for eighteen months and did his share of the work of clearing rubble from Allied bombing raids.

When word spread of their heroism, a reporter came to our refugee camp at Wildflecken, Germany, to interview Fr. Marian. He asked Fr. Marian about how they saved Mitch's life. Fr. Marian replied, "I don't think you understand. We didn't save his life; he saved ours. He gave us the reason to keep going."

They are my heroes and perfect examples of what it means to be Christian. Fr. Marian was our pastor in Wildflecken and remained our dear friend in the U.S. He was pastor of St. Casimir Church in Streator, Illinois, until his death of a stroke in about 1974..

Acknowledgements

My deepest gratitude to my loving wife, Rosemarie, whose unflagging support, proof reading, editing, and endless patience made it possible to devote many hours to the task.

I am indebted to my mentors, Dr. Marvin E. Mundel, Evan Scheele, and Irving Footlik, all heads of consulting firms with which I was associated. Dr. Willard Carter first saw my potential and took time to teach me his craft. Ted Busch, technical writer, taught me to write concisely and allowed me to ghost write trade magazine articles for him. Ian McNiven hired me, a kid without a college degree, against company policy. Meyer (Mike) and Norma Ragir, whose confidence in me allowed me to rise into senior management of their company.

Many of them are long gone, but they shall always live in my memory.

Preface

My previous book on socioeconomics, *MegaMyths of Politics, Economics, and Religion* by Eugene Schwarz, included numerous tables, charts, facts, and statistics aimed at enhancing people's understanding of economics and critical socioeconomic issues. Those who read it gave it high praise, but it failed to start a movement. If more had read it carefully and understood it, they would have been alarmed at the warning bells that rang from its pages.

It is not the objective of this book to merely grumble about the problems in our society, but to offer effective solutions. My back ground includes more than a decade as a management consultant turning around troubled companies by improving methods and implementing well-integrated systems. That was followed by two and a half decades in senior management of two companies, one international and one domestic. The analytical and systems engineering skills I developed have served me well in business and my personal life. I trust you will find that they would also serve to fix the financial, political, and social systems in our nation. Words alone will not get it done. All of us working together with a common vision can.

"You write in order to change the world, knowing perfectly well that you probably can't, but also knowing that literature is indispensable to the world... The world changes according to the way people see it, and if you alter, even by a millimeter, the way ... people look at reality, then you can change it."

James Arthur Baldwin (1924-1987), American writer, poet, civil rights activist.

Contents

WAKE UP! 1

ONE VOTER, ONE VOICE, ONE VOTE 13

A FAIR TAX 19

A LIVING WAGE 29

SAVING OUR MONEY 35

RETIREMENT SECURITY 43

HEALTH CARE 49

IMMIGRATION 59

NO CHILD LEFT BEHIND 73

RACE TO SPACE 105

FREEDOM OF RELIGION 123

THE SECOND AMENDMENT 139

CRIMINAL JUSTICE 149

FREEDOM OF SPEECH 161

GOVERNMENT OF, BY, FOR PEOPLE 167

CONCLUSION 171

Author Biography 173

History will have to record that the greatest tragedy of this period of social transition was not the strident clamor of the bad people, but the appalling silence of the good people.

Martin Luther King Jr quotes

WAKE UP!

In about 250 BC, the Greek philosopher Eratosthenes conducted an experiment that proved that the earth was a globe and calculated its circumference quite accurately. Nevertheless, it took another 1800 years for people to begin to give up their false belief that the earth was a pancake shaped object at the center of the universe, which was based on an incorrect interpretation of the Bible. Galileo had proof that Eratosthenes was correct, but the authorities would not even look at it. He avoided being burned at the stake by agreeing not to promote his findings.

One of my early mentors was Dr. Marvin Mundel, head of industrial engineering at Purdue University. He conducted a number of experiments in his classroom intended to demonstrate the importance of proper data collection and analysis in solving problems, determining the true cause of a problem before attempting to solve it.

In one such experiment, there were three lines drawn on the blackboard at the front of the class. Two of the lines were identical in length, while one was slightly longer. The lines were marked A, B, and C. The students were asked to each state which line was the longest. Several of the most influential students were secretly asked to intentionally give the same incorrect answer. About one-third of the remaining students gave the same incorrect answer. We are like herd animals in a stampede, even when the lead bull is heading for a cliff. One student held up a pencil in both hands and positioned his fingers in line with the ends of each line on the blackboard. Sighting across them, he could easily determine which line was the longest. That little bit of data collection helped him to see the truth.

In another experiment, students were each given two pieces of paper as they entered the room. Each student was identified with a unique number on each piece of paper. A projector was turned on displaying a blurred image on a screen. Each student was asked to identify the object in the image as soon as able and to write it on one paper along with the time on the classroom wall clock. Each minute the focus adjustment was increased slightly. Students who changed their minds were to repeat the process on the second piece of paper. It should be no surprise that, when the results were charted, those who were first to make an incorrect identification were always last to identify the object (a fire hydrant) correctly. There was simply too little available data upon which to base identification when the object was completely blurred.

As this is being written, Pew Research published a finding that 78% of people say that they not only disagree on plans and policies, but on basic facts. In this day and age of alternative facts, it has become increasingly difficult to determine what the truth is on the most important issues. Political parties have coalesced around diametrically opposed ideologies neither of which has delivered a fair and equitable society. The problem is not with the people in government and their intentions. It is with the system. Their words say that we are a capitalist democracy, but their actions prove that we are neither.

Democracy is based on the will of the people and capitalism is based on open markets and competition. If we were either, would our Medicare prescription drug plan be prevented from negotiating prices? Would we not rather be free to buy them on the global market — the same places the pharmaceutical companies buy drugs and components for drugs? Would our Social Security premiums be transferred to the general fund, spent, and replaced with bonds that can only pay interest by stealing from future premium payments? These, like many of our systems, are actually designed to fail.

Banks can charge us any interest they want although they can borrow our money from the Federal Reserve for near to nothing, so they pay us nothing for our savings. Should they not be paying us a fair share of their profits for the use of our money? How else can most people ever save money for retirement?

How is it possible in a global economy that a corporation that gets much or most of its revenue from the United States can register itself in Ireland and pay no U.S. income taxes? Or for more than thirteen thousand U.S. corporations to be registered in the Cayman Islands alone?

Businesses have fought to undermine labor unions while forming their own unions as trade associations to funnel money to lobbyists to buy votes for bills favorable to their industries. They must get enough benefit from such spending to justify doing it.

Perhaps we should not be too harsh on the politicians who benefit from their largess. They are only trying to keep their jobs. In an era of billion dollar political campaigns, a U.S. congressman, with only a two year term, must spend virtually his or her entire term fundraising to be reelected. The problem is in the system.

The Supreme Court has exacerbated the problem by confusing free speech with money. It has raised the cost of elections by allowing special interest money to flow from undisclosed sources, including foreign sources, into political action committees, into political advertising, to political parties, and even directly to politicians. What right should the government of one country have to influence elections in another or a billionaire from one state to influence elections in another? Or, for that matter, should non-voting entities (such as unions, trade associations, charitable institutions, churches, and political action committees) be entitled to do so? Just today it was reported that a political action committee allied with Mitch McConnell donated $25 million to his senatorial reelection campaign. They are not charitable institutions. What do they expect to get for their money? Should I be surprised that my $25 contribution does not get me any special attention?

How much voice does a minimum wage worker have? Congress has not raised the federal minimum wage in nine years, leaving it at $7.25 per hour. A one bedroom apartment rents for approximately $1,000 per month. Even working 40 hours per week, 173 hours per month, $5.77 per hour would only pay the rent. The remaining $1.48 would not cover food and transportation to work (even if public transportation was available), much less health insurance and other necessities. Why else would young people live with parents into their thirties or in group living arrangements that often result in fractured families?

Do you wonder why we have so much welfare, Mr. and Ms. Senator or Representative? You created it by failing to lift people out of poverty by clinging to outdated and ineffective ideologies. Rent subsidies go to the landlords, food stamps go to the food suppliers, Medicaid costs go to health care providers, heating subsidies go to the energy companies, etc. They do nothing to lift people out of poverty therefore they guarantee we will have many poor working people and many homeless.

You are also complicit in causing the 2007-2008 financial crisis. In 1999 you enacted the Gramm Leach Bliley Act that dismantled the Glass Steagal Act that protected the financial industry for decades. It prevented insurance companies and commercial banks, those who make their money from lending, from engaging in investment banking. That allowed insurance companies to gamble with our premiums and commercial banks to gamble with our savings. In 2000 you passed the Commodity Futures Trading Modernization Act. It allowed swaps to be traded as commodities. Was it not predatory lending protected by credit default swaps that ns that ghastly wound with the Frank Dodd Act. It provided for the dismantling and selloff of insolvent banks. The question is "To whom?". Who but insurance companies and big banks have the resources to buy them? Does that not just make them "too big to fail", forcing us to bail them out when they do?

Many point to the current economic boom (growth in Gross Domestic Product, GDP) as affirmation of President Trump's policies. The simple formula for **GDP** is **Government Spending Plus Personal Spending**. The boom is fueled by unsustainable massive deficit spending by the government. We only recovered from the Great Depression when World War II spending reduced unemployment to almost zero. During the Vietnam War unemployment fell to 3.2%. The recession of 1982-86 took unemployment from 10.8% to less than 5% only after the Reagan Administration spent hundreds of billions of dollars with military contractors on the Star Wars program. The George W. Bush administration spent fortunes on the wars in Iraq, Afghanistan, and the War on Terror, much of which continues to be spent each year. We are all still paying for a century of wars and military buildups, leaving little left for other essentials. Only a fool would think we won't have to pay for it. The choices will be bankruptcy or massive inflation. You can decide which will be better for you.

Few individuals or corporations can provide adequate health care. Health insurance costs make corporations non-competitive with those that do not provide health care coverage, or even with the same kind of corporations in nations with universal health care systems. If the citizens of those countries are happy with their health care, the cost is substantially less than what it costs us, the outcomes are often better, and the health facilities are privately owned, what excuse can you possibly have for keeping it from us, except a twisted ideology?

You might scream "Socialism!" to scare us, but you won't scare me. I was born under Soviet occupation of Eastern Poland, now Ukraine. The USSR (Union of Soviet Socialist Republics) was soon replaced by the Nazis (National Socialists) of Germany. The USSR took possession of all land, housing, and businesses. The Nazis took whatever they wanted from those of non-German ethnicity. Both took the lives and fortunes of many millions of people, including their own citizens. Two of my sisters died in one year because the Russians sent most of the Polish Jewish and gentile doctors to Kazakhstan and Siberia, shutting down health care completely.

WAKE UP! 9

My family and I certainly did not get any health care in Auschwitz or the Dachau satellite camp we were subsequently transferred to by the Nazis, even though they disabled me for eighteen months. That is the kind of socialism I fear. Hitler and Stalin were megalomaniacs and ideologues whose ideology was more important to them than their people. What about your ideology?

We are immigrants like most of your ancestors. I was born not far from where Caucasians originated. We came here to escape communism and to live the American dream. My cousins who returned to Soviet era Poland did not nearly fare so well. We came as refugees at a more enlightened time. I would not be so dismayed at your failure to deal with the illegal immigration problem if the solution were not so simple. The wall is not it.

The lessons I learned from Marvin Mundel and other key mentors served me well over the years. I honed my analytical skills as a consultant turning around troubled businesses. I found that most of those businesses lacked a clear strategic plan and employed ineffective systems and methods. I improved productivity by implementing efficient methods and integrating systems to work smoothly together. I have applied my analytical skills to the most serious socioeconomic issues to see if system engineering principles can be applied to develop integrated solutions.

My previous book on socioeconomic issues, *MegaMyths of Politics, Economics, and Religion* by Eugene Schwarz, was full of tables and charts aimed at explaining the causes of the crises we face. While some readers found it enlightening, it failed to start a movement. Apparently the amount of information was more than many could process, so I decided this book had to be short, on point, based on logic and common sense, and focus on solutions. I also changed my pen name to E. J. Schwarz to avoid being confused with another author named Eugene Schwarz whose books were mostly fiction.

While I have addressed much of the foregoing to Senators and Representatives in Congress, I realize that they are so mired in their respective ideologies that they will probably ignore anything that differs from theirs. I sent letters outlining some potential solutions to all Senators and all leaders in the House of Representatives of both parties. I received a response from only one of them, Michael Bennett, first an acknowledgement and then a follow-up letter. He is the only one who I am sure to support.

WAKE UP!

My hope is that my message will resonate with the American people and that they will apply so much pressure on the politicians that they will be forced take steps to save the America I love.

"If liberty and equality, as is thought by some, are chiefly to be found in democracy, they will be best attained when all persons alike share in government to the utmost."

Aristotle (384-322 BC), ancient Greek philosopher.

Progress is impossible without change, and those who cannot change their minds cannot change anything.

George Bernard Shaw (1856-1950), Irish writer.

Voting is our right, but it is also our responsibility because if we don't take the next step and elect leaders who are committed to building a better future for our kids, other rights — our rights to clean air, clean water, health, and prosperity — are placed directly in harm's way.

Tom Steyer

ONE VOTER, ONE VOICE, ONE VOTE

Marvin Mundel taught me through his many classroom experiments how easily minds can be manipulated and therefore how important the collection of evidence is before forming opinions. Most of us have one voice with which we can communicate our opinions. A billionaire has greater access to a variety of media personally, through businesses he or she owns, their industry associations, the lobbyists they employ, and the political action committees they support. The Supreme Court, in its worst possible decision in its history, has ruled that money is speech, in essence drowning out my voice. The result has been that the cost of political campaigns has skyrocketed, money is allowed to pour in from undisclosed sources, the airwaves are jammed with negative political advertizing, and Congress seems oblivious to the will of the people. Money can buy speech, but money is not speech.

Only individual voters should be allowed to make political contributions and only to candidates in elections in which that individual is permitted to vote. Someone in a foreign country must not affect elections in the United States, and someone in a particular state must not affect elections in another state. All political contributions must be fully disclosed to make sure the contributor and the recipient are both in the same jurisdiction as the office for which the election is being held.

This also means that unions, corporations, industry associations, churches, institutions, organizations, and political action committees would likewise be prohibited from making political contributions. The one exception would be that political parties could support their candidates and candidates could elect to split their contributions with their parties if they so choose.

It also means that those prohibited from making political contributions must also be prohibited from political advertising. We the people must recognize that the candidate will be working for us if elected, and that the election campaign is his or her job interview. We must demand that the candidate explain to us how he or she will address our concerns and needs and what qualifies that candidate for the position. I have hired many people in my career as a senior executive in an international company. I never hired one who spent the interview bashing his former employers or coworkers. Neither should you hire the candidate who spends his time bashing other candidates. Since only the candidate and his party will be permitted to advertize for the candidate, we will be better able to judge their character.

In the earliest days of our republic, most members of the House were part timers with other occupations. Serving for two years would have allowed them to get back to earning a living. Those days are never coming back. Now a two year term only guarantees that virtually their entire term will be spent fundraising for their reelection. No wonder they can't get anything done. I believe a **four year term** would significantly increase the productivity of Congress and reduce spending on campaigns.

By shutting off money from lobbyists, Congress would be free to solicit input from experts in various fields related to bills under consideration. It would put oil industry executives, scientists, and environmentalists on an equal footing when lobbyist money is no longer on the table. Raising the pay of representatives might also help them resist the influence of money under the table.

We tend to value most highly those representatives who **bring home the most bacon** (pork) to our states. They do so by requesting money for various projects in their home states by attaching the requests, called

earmarks, to various bills going through congress. In many cases, the earmarks are attached to bills having nothing at all to do with subject matter of the bills. This makes it virtually impossible to establish fiscal responsibility. Many of the projects are not bid competitively, may be intended to benefit political supporters, or may not be needed at all. It is long past time to establish a proper budgeting process. States should submit their requests to Congress in priority order categorized (transportation, education, health care, research, etc.) for easy incorporation into a master budget. All such projects should be competitively bid and be approved by the voters of their state. I am relatively certain the voters would not approve a study of the sex life of ants (low value), or the building of a parking garage in Provo, Utah, (a purely local matter). The federal government should only support state expenditures that promote the wellbeing of its citizens, facilitate interstate commerce, and are in the national interest. Except for responding to disasters beyond the capability of individual states, the federal government should not otherwise be involved in strictly local matters. How much any one state gets should never be based upon the clout wielded by its representatives, but by the state's needs. Every bill passing through

Congress should be able to stand on its own merits free of earmarks or provisions unrelated to the subject of the bill. That is the only way we can be sure a good solution was found by consultation with experts instead of arm twisting. It would also do much to reduce the cost of government.

In the 2000 and 2004 elections, voting irregularities with punch card ballots and electronic machines created some concern about accuracy of vote counts. In 2016 hacking attempts and disinformation campaigns by Russian intelligence agents threatened to disrupt our voting system. The voter has no means of ascertaining that the vote has not been tampered with or the machines hacked. Democracy depends on every person's vote counting. That requires positive identification of voters and means of verifying their vote. That is why there must be a paper trail. Most of us cannot remember how we voted on every issue and for every position. We should receive a printout of our vote from the voting machine. Our votes should be transmitted electronically to the Federal Election Commission to serve as a crosscheck. Then a postcard documenting our vote, coded for privacy, should be sent us in the mail. That would allow us to compare the vote we cast to the vote as it was counted.

Perhaps the fact that we have seen millions voting themselves into complete dependence on a tyrant has made our generation understand that to choose one's government is not necessarily to secure freedom.

Friedrich August von Hayek

For some reason, voters can be brainwashed, and they vote sometimes against their own best interests, let alone voting against the interests of people who need them, like people who are disenfranchised and people who are poor and so forth.

Joyce Carol Oates

A FAIR TAX

Hardly anyone believes that our system of taxation is fair. Most people have no idea how much of their income goes to taxes, what taxes they are paying, and who is paying most of them. When we consider all forms of taxation, like state income taxes, property taxes, sales taxes, vehicle license fees, utility taxes, excise taxes, entertainment taxes, tolls, duties, etc., they exceed what we pay in federal income taxes. Politicians love user-based taxes because they are easier to pass. All taxes on products and services get passed through to the consumer. Because they are applied at the point of sale, they are perceived as product cost, so consumers rarely complain. Don't be misled; they are taxes, and they must be paid even when one has little or no income. You are paying far more in taxes than you ever imagined. We have been told that the reason is entitlements like Social Security and Medicare. That is partially true, but they are large enough issues to deserve separate chapters. For now, we will address the tax system itself.

All government spending comes from taxes, either money collected from you each year or borrowed from investors to be repaid with interest in the future by you, your children, and their children, in perpetuity.

Before currency was invented and most societies were agrarian, most business was done by barter. People's livestock, produce, and labor were the only basis for collecting taxes. One could be wealthy without having money as such. Today, that is no longer the case, but property taxes continue to be levied. Because they are community based, the wealthiest communities have excellent schools and services, while the poorer, which are far greater in number, receive the bare minimum. The property tax is usually hidden in a mortgage or rent payment, so we sometimes forget that it is a tax. Worst of all, it doesn't care whether the taxpayer had any income at all. Some states have exorbitant vehicle license fees based on the value of the vehicle. This is just another property tax. The sixty year old person who cannot find a job, whose unemployment compensation has run out, and who is still too young to collect social security, must nevertheless pay his property tax or lose his home or his car. After a lifetime of good citizenship and taxpaying, that is hardly fair.

A FAIR TAX

Most state and local tax revenues come from hidden taxes affecting those most whose earnings go primarily for living costs — those on disability, social security, or other fixed incomes. Sales, value added, or consumption taxes are also unfair because they do not take into account a person's ability to pay. Corporations pay very little in state and local taxes, so they want most government responsibilities handled at the state level.

None of the tax reforms proposed in recent years do anything to correct the fundamental problem: that gross revenues (money received) of corporations is nearly three times that of individuals, yet they pay a small fraction of what individuals pay in taxes. They can deduct nearly all of their expenses while individuals can only deduct a portion of their most essential expenses. The resulting savings increases the wealth of stockholders and chief executives, which is only taxed at the much smaller capital gains rate, but it does not increase the workers' pay.

Taxing based on profits is ridiculous because profits are not easily verifiable, even by experts. That makes enforcement difficult, and forces government to get involved in the minutiae of a business or household budget. Complex rules and regulations lead to inevitable loopholes and make it difficult to catch tax cheats. Much revenue is lost to under-reporting of income and use of tax shelters and sophisticated tax avoidance schemes, among the most egregious of which is registering one's company in a tax haven like the Cayman Islands, just to name one. Apple Corporation, the first U.S. company to achieve a valuation of $1 trillion registered itself in Ireland and so pays no U.S. income tax. Many other Fortune 500 companies also pay little or nothing in U.S. taxes. In a global economy, every corporation is a citizen of the world, not of a tax haven. We must rid ourselves of this insane system.

You may not be aware of it, but if a corporation loses money, you will pay to make them whole. If you look at the annual reports of corporations that lost money in a given year, you will find that the after tax loss is considerably smaller than the pretax loss. Who do you think made up much of that loss? You did!

The time has come to face reality. Individual income is an inadequate tax base to meet our national needs. In an increasingly global economy, we must develop a system of taxation that is independent of the country or state of incorporation or location of facilities. It cannot

A FAIR TAX

be based on profits because they are not easily verifiable, encourage cheating, and invite government intrusion into business operations and personal lives. It must not discriminate on the basis of marital status or number of dependents. It must not give preferential treatment on the basis of type of corporation, organization, or association. Furthermore, it must be totally free of subsidies, exemptions, exclusions, and deductions. It must apply only one tax rate to all individuals and entities regardless of income level or profit. Finally, it must be simple, understandable, and enforceable. I call it a gross revenues tax or GRT.

My proposal requires the elimination of all forms of taxation except one — **a single flat rate income tax on gross receipts of all individuals, corporations, and organizations without exception, payable to the country and state from which money is received, with no exemptions, deductions, exclusions, or subsidies, and no place to hide. I estimate that a GRT federal tax rate of 8% and a state tax rate of 6% would cover all government spending without deficits.**

Of course, there would be an immediate increase in prices, but it would be accompanied by an immediate and proportional increase in aggregate disposable income. Setting prices is not the role of government or individual taxpayers. Businesses must set prices sufficient to be competitive, make a profit, and pay their taxes. As long as all foreign and domestic businesses pay taxes to the countries and states from which they receive money, and there are no subsidies of any kind, no nation, state, or business has an unfair advantage over any other. The most efficient businesses and governments would benefit most. Extremely low individual taxes would promote entrepreneurship, business formation, and jobs, especially in less skilled occupations where the need is greatest. Because taxes would be directly proportional to prices, industries that gouge the public would repay the public by contributing more in taxes. Corporations that set up manufacturing operations in other countries would pay tax on goods shipped into the U.S. just like foreign corporations on their sales to us.

To avoid any unintended consequences, the transition must be made slowly to allow time for adjustment. A ten-year period should be adequate. Each year, the current tax for every form of taxation and all subsidies would be reduced by ten percent from the original, and the gross receipts tax would increase by ten percent.

A FAIR TAX

The economic impact would become apparent after the first year.

The process would temporarily add two lines to a tax return. At the end of the conversion period, tax returns could be as simple as two to four lines. In fact for many no tax return would be required since employers could simply send the employees' withheld tax money to the IRS electronically each month. The annual tax return would be for supplemental income. Much of the information the government currently collects by separate forms for numerous agencies can be inferred from a one-page tax return, and then distributed to the appropriate agencies. The savings for businesses and government alike would be substantial. It might even be possible to replace the census taking process by incorporating it into a mandatory tax return. Paying one's income tax monthly in proportion to revenue would eliminate the financial shock many of us experience annually and eliminate the burdensome data collection process.

It would probably require a constitutional amendment to limit the ability of Congress to grant exemptions or subsidies, pass new taxes, or increase the tax rate, except temporarily in times of war or national emergency. It should also require states to similarly limit the power of their legislatures and only tax on gross revenues. Getting other nations to agree might be difficult, but if the world's largest economy did it, others would follow suit if only in retaliation.

Two industries would require somewhat different treatment than most. The money deposited by clients in financial institutions is held for the clients' benefit, and should not be taxed. All other financial institution receipts that are not customer deposits should be taxed at the flat rate. Like financial institutions, insurance company premiums are held for the benefit of the insured. Any receipts in excess of claim payments should be taxed at the flat rate.

Any tax reform scheme must be understandable and agreeable to the populace and the business community for it to succeed in the long term. I have tried to anticipate some of the questions that might arise, and to provide concise answers. It is my fervent hope you will see the benefits:

- Reduced cost of living for most people.
- A larger tax base makes it possible to eliminate deficits and reduce the national debt.
- The charade of raiding the Social Security and other funds to reduce deficits goes away when all government obligations are paid from the general fund.

A FAIR TAX

- Less bureaucracy. The IRS would be free to concentrate on investigation and collection in an environment that makes cheating extremely difficult.
- We would not need to hire tax experts to do our tax returns.
- Accountants would be free to concentrate on business profits, and helping people to manage their resources.
- Everyone would understand the tax codes, so the level of frustration would be dramatically reduced.
- There would be no opportunity for politicians to give special consideration to special interests.
- Government budgets and reports would be more intelligible for the layman.
- Equal treatment of rich and poor would reduce the tension between them.
- Equal treatment of corporations and individuals would become practical.
- Lower personal taxes would encourage the creation of new businesses.
- Businesses which make the most efficient use of materials, services, and labor would pay the lowest taxes and retain the highest profits.
- Equal treatment of domestic and foreign corporations would minimize the advantage they now have over domestic businesses.
- Free trade without duties or tariffs would become practical.

- The use of tax havens like the Cayman Islands to facilitate global commerce becomes unnecessary.
- The system allows true capitalism. Since taxes would be equal for all products and services, competition would be based on merit, marketing skill, and demand.

As you can see, the GRT reduces income taxes on all individuals including the wealthiest therefore it promotes a healthy economy by putting more money in people's hands. While I believe that high progressive tax rates are unfair, the notion that they kill businesses and therefore jobs is a myth. The greatest economic expansion in the United States occurred during the two decades following World War II. Computers, jet aircraft, nuclear power, space exploration, television, home appliances, housing, automobiles, farming, food production, credit cards, and myriad other industries experienced dramatic growth and innovation while the top income tax rate on the wealthiest individuals was 91-92%. They invested heavily in research and development to create new products and services to increase the value of their companies.

Taxes are the price of civilization.
Oliver Wendell Holmes Jr. (1841- 1935), Associate Justice of the U.S. Supreme Court

A LIVING WAGE

A few years ago, I read that the federal government, in attempting to set the Federal Poverty Guideline while trying to meet federal nutritional guidelines, was forced to find nutritional equivalents because the guideline could not be set low enough if red meat was included in the diet. Perhaps they thought that if cattle can prosper eating grass and living outdoors, people could as well. That appears to be the logic they used when the current poverty guidelines were set:

$12,060 for 1 person, $16,240 for 2, $20,420 for 3, $24,600 for 4

What planet were they living on? I challenge any one member of Congress to survive one year on any of those numbers without assistance. They might answer with, "That's why we created many assistance programs to help the poor." Really? Then why are there still so many homeless and working poor? Clearly, welfare is not the answer. If people can make more money begging on street corners, why work?

Henry David Thoreau once said "Most men lead lives of quiet desperation and go to the grave with the song still in them." All too often I have heard someone say that there are no really poor people in America. They point to countries in Africa or South America where people are 'really poor.' The truth is that no one will let you build a mud hut, dig a well, cut firewood, plant a garden, or hunt for food year-round on land you do not own. We will not allow a witch doctor to practice medicine. We have built a society where the poor must pay for lodging, heat, electricity, water, food, health care, and transportation. It is a different type of poverty, but it is poverty nonetheless, a poverty of perpetual debt. The only relief seems to be in drink or drugs.

The reason we cannot see it is illustrated in this true story from two of my business trips in the early 1980's. Remarkably, both men involved were named Tony. Hong Kong was inundated with approximately 600,000 refugees from communist China and Viet Nam. They built shacks of bamboo, cardboard, and any scrap of material they could find, on top of buildings and any vacant piece of land. One such shantytown rose to three levels on a small park, about three acres in size. As we were driving past it, I asked, "Tony, is this where the poor people live?" He responded, "There are no poor people in Hong Kong. You should see them arriving downtown in their Mercedes cars to go begging." Two months later, I was in Portugal, driving north from Lisbon. Looking to the west, I saw a shantytown that, aside from being one level, looked very much like the one in Hong Kong. I turned to the second Tony and asked, "Tony, is this where the poor people live?" He responded, "There are no poor people in Portugal. You should see them arriving in their Mercedes cars to go begging in downtown Lisbon." There were no roads, no garages, and no vehicle tracks.

Each of them may have seen a beggar getting out of a Mercedes. Certainly, there are a few scam artists among beggars. Or, perhaps some kind wealthy person had given them a lift. Admitting that there were real poor might place a sense of guilt upon them, so they block the very thought from their minds. They sincerely believe that everyone has the same opportunity as they had and that their poverty is their own fault, so they don't deserve help and should not be asking for it.

Most of us form opinions on this matter with no evidence or experience. I had the privilege of coordinating a program for the homeless in which our church participated in the Chicago area. We provided part time shelter, food, and bathing/laundry facilities for individuals and families. Over four years, I watched competent professionals, divorced families, seniors, young people, ex-convicts, and others struggle against mental illness caused by the stress of their situation. A few of those I counseled and assisted were able to find jobs and return to a more normal life, but most required help beyond anything I could offer.

Imagine yourself with no address, no telephone, clean clothes, or place to bathe, only one duffel bag of belongings, and no money. How would you prepare a resume and post it on a jobs website? How would they contact you if they wanted to interview you? How would you get there? How would you make yourself presentable? How would you pass a drug test? Finally, if they hired you, how would you get there? Would the pay they are offering be enough for housing and other living costs? If your mental or physical state must be controlled with medication, will you be able to pay for it? The odds against getting out of that trap are overwhelming.

We need transitional services to help people out of poverty, addictions, incarceration, and natural and accidental catastrophes. If these services do not provide housing, comprehensive health care, job training, communications, and transportation, they will not be able to rescue them. We provide most of these services to rescue pets. Why not human? What's the

A LIVING WAGE

alternative, incarceration? We already incarcerate more people and spend far more to do it than any other country in the world.

As difficult as it is to get out of trouble, it is even more difficult to stay out. That's where you come in. You can provide a living wage by increasing the minimum wage to a level that reflects a realistic poverty level in this country. Enable young people to pay for their education without incurring decades of massive debt that prevents them from saving for retirement. Enable them all to pay into the health care system so that they will have affordable health care as they age and need more of it. Enable everyone to have adequate nutrition and recreational activity for maintaining good health. Adjust the minimum wage annually by the increase in the consumer price index to keep them from sliding back into poverty. It will also keep the minimum wage from continuing to be a political football. If you calculate a budget covering the essentials, you will realize that $14 per hour for all workers will suffice in all states but those with the highest cost of living.

Don't believe the nonsense that higher wages will cause job loss. All past minimum wage increases were followed by job gains. Business is fueled by people with money to spend. The increased cost is often offset by reduced training costs, increased efficiency, and better quality due to lower employee turnover rates. At the national and state level, it will significantly reduce welfare cost.

Capitalists are supposed to resist redistribution of wealth, but you have instead redistributed wealth upward to the already rich. As a word of caution, the great depression of the 1930s began with a top tax rate of 25%, the lowest in the last century, and the greatest inequality in wealth. We have now surpassed that milestone.

People from both political parties have long recognized that welfare without work creates negative incentives that lead to permanent poverty. It robs people of self-esteem.

Mitt Romney, 2012 U.S. Presidential candidate

SAVING OUR MONEY

In the 1950s, many high schools offered home economics courses teaching essential life skills. It taught young people how to save and manage money, balance a checkbook, prepare a household budget, buy wisely, buy and prepare foods that provide proper nutrition, and myriad other subjects that prepared them for independence. With increasing pressure from an increasingly powerful financial sector, these programs soon disappeared from our educational system. Apparently they wanted to keep us stupid so they got you to pass laws the effects of which we would not understand.

At various points in our history, economic activity was driven by agriculture, industry, services, and information. Now it is dominated by the FIRE sector (finance, insurance, and real estate), which represents about forty percent of our economy. It is a fitting acronym for a sector that nearly burned down the economy of the entire world.

In 1982, the Reagan Administration enacted the Depository Institutions Act that removed interest rate ceilings and limits on loan to value ratios. It also gave banks greater flexibility to invest in riskier ventures. Over the next six years more than 1300 banks failed. A $600 billion government bailout prevented an even greater crisis. If Congress wanted to be fair, that bill would have provided that depositors would be paid a proportionate share of interest income for the use of their money.

In 1933, during the great depression, 4000 banks failed. To slow the collapse, Congress passed the Glass Steagall Act and created the Federal Deposit Insurance Corporation (FDIC) to protect depositors against bank failures. The number of bank failures declined from 4000 in 1933 to 57 in 1934. Bank failures increased again under deregulation in the 1980s and again in 2007-2010. In fact, most domestic financial crises in more than a century were precipitated by failures in unregulated segments of the financial sector: trusts in 1907, investment banks in 1929-1933, deregulated savings and loans in the 1980s, and the shadow banking system (money market) more recently. In the aftermath of the last crisis an FDIC-like program was proposed for investment banks but was rejected under industry pressure. It is difficult to understand why the FIRE sector would want deregulation when it leads to bank failures. The only explanation can be that big banks grow bigger by absorbing the business of failing banks.

In 1999, Congress passed the Gramm-Leach-Bliley Act, repealing the Glass-Steagall Act and further deregulating the banking industry. The lines between commercial banks, investment banks, and insurance companies blurred, and some banks grew so large that the failure of one or two could bring down the entire economy. Reinstating something akin to the Glass Steagall Act was proposed and should have been enacted, but financial industry pressure forced it to be dropped. Two presidential candidates in the 2016 election vowed to reinstate an updated version of that bill, but they did not win.

That is unfortunate because it will be extremely difficult to save Social Security and Medicare, balance the national budget, and save banking for the long term unless we do reinstate it. You will have to wait for the next chapter to understand why that is true. For now, let's try to understand what is wrong with the current system.

When insurance companies, commercial banks, and investment banks combine, your savings and insurance premiums can be used to gamble on risky investments. Most homeowners have experienced their home mortgage being repeatedly sold and resold. The mortgages are bundled and securitized. Riskier mortgages impose higher interest rates than safer ones, so there is no incentive for the lender to seek safe borrowers and no incentive for the lender to retain the mortgage until it is paid off. The mortgage is sold off and the money is used to lend to other risky borrowers. The lender has no skin in the game. Only the homeowner and the investor are at risk. Smaller community banks have no access to the revolving money tray, so they must lend to creditworthy borrowers and hold onto the mortgages. That limits the amount of capital they can devote to home mortgages and other lending.

Insurance companies are banks of sorts. We deposit our premiums in them so that in the event of accident, illness, or natural disaster, we can be made whole. In recent years, insurance companies have held controlling shares in several major investment banks. That allows them to invest our premium money for their own accounts and fund buybacks of their own stocks. They have no incentive to keep premium costs and payouts low because they are cost-plus businesses. Any failed investments are at our expense. In order for our money not to lose value due to inflation, it can be deposited in commercial banks to earn interest.

Prior to the stock market crash of 1929, before regulations were imposed to prevent such activities, banks were using depositors' money to invest in risky issues. Poorly secured loans were issued to companies in which banks had invested, and the banks' clients were advised to invest in the debtor companies while the banks were short selling those stocks. During the financial crisis of 2007-2008, Goldman Sachs, a global investment banking firm, was fined $550 million for allegedly advising customers to buy certain securities while themselves short selling them. **Investment banks should not trade for their own account.** They are, in fact, acting as our agents. We pay them a commission on trades or a management fee. If they advise us to buy a certain security, they should only benefit further if we benefit. The mission of investment banks is to increase wealth, not destroy it, therefore **short sales should be outlawed**.

One might ask, "How can they make enough money just from commissions and management fees to stay afloat?" The answer is, "By underwriting initial public offerings (IPO) in profitable companies with growth potential." In an IPO, the firm or firms underwriting a stock gets a certain percent share of the stock to sell for its own account, thereby building up its cash reserves. It can also deposit its money in commercial; banks to earn interest.

Economists estimate that stock buy-backs will exceed $1 trillion this year, which is where much of the recent windfall from tax cuts has gone. The purpose of the stock market is to bring in investors to enable corporations to increase their revenues through new products and services, and their profits through improved technologies and systems. Insurance companies are among the guiltiest buyers back of their own stock. It takes our premium payments to drive up the price of its own stock, which results in huge bonuses to chief executives, higher insurance prices, and less money available for providing benefits. It is happening across many industries. It causes price inflation (reducing the value of people's money) without increasing wages or benefits. We must recognize that stock buy backs by insurance companies and other corporations harm the consumer and do nothing to enhance the economy, although there is occasionally a practical reason for a buy-back. When a company is otherwise successful, but its stock price fails to bring in sufficient investment, a company might choose to take itself private, in which case it must publicly commit to do so and the stock price must be frozen as of that date to prevent investors from driving the stock price up to a level that would prevent privatization of the company or short sell the stock to drive it into bankruptcy. Another reason for a buy-back is when investors' demands on a business are not in its long term strategic interest, which is often the case.

Also destructive to an economy is the short sale. A short sale allows an investor to sell a large amount of a particular stock that he or she does not actually own, but merely borrows from the investment firm. The sale drives down the stock price and therefore the valuation of the company whose stock is being sold, sometimes driving it into bankruptcy. ? Just this month, Elon Musk, the brilliant CEO of Tesla Motors and Space X, was complaining that short sellers were endangering Tesla. He threatened to take the company private. Some years ago a major investor sold short about $10 billion of British pounds, nearly destroying the value of that currency. No one allows me to borrow and sell their property, unless I buy that property first. Was Congress asleep or have they been bought

We cannot completely ban risky behavior in investments. One can buy shares in a hedge fund that only trades for its own account, but hedge funds should not be affiliated with any investment bank, commercial bank, or insurance company, except that it could deposit its cash in commercial banks.

Banks should be required to **prevent the devaluation of our money by paying interest on our deposits equivalent to at least 25% of the interest and fees it charges us**. It is time to make us savers again. They won't do it unless you make it a law.

One way we can assure creditworthiness of borrowers is to have all lending activity handled by commercial banks. **Since credit card purchases are in fact short term loans, only commercial banks should be allowed to issue credit cards.**

Finally, Congress must find some way to rein in the abuses by the pay day lenders and check cashing services who charge outrageous interest and fees.

"Curst greed of gold, what crimes thy tyrant power has caused"
Virgil (70 BC–19 BC), ancient Roman poet

RETIREMENT SECURITY

My wife and I were having lunch with friends at a local restaurant after church one Sunday a few years ago when our conversation turned to politics. One presidential candidate had spoken of eliminating entitlements. A couple in an adjoining booth, about our age, decided to join the conversation. The man said, "We ought to get rid of entitlements." I asked him, "So, you want to quit getting a Social Security check?" He quickly responded, "No." I followed up with, "Then, you must want to give up Medicare, and buy your own health insurance?" Again he responded, "No." That led me to ask, "So, exactly which entitlements do you want to get rid of?" The puzzled look on his face told me he had fallen for the political rhetoric without understanding the implications. To many people, entitlements are what everyone else gets. Hardly anyone wants to lose their Social Security or Medicare. That has forced some politicians to redefine 'getting rid of entitlements' to its exact opposite, 'saving Social Security.' That leads to another question: "Why does Social Security need saving?"

We have all heard that the problem is an aging population – people living longer – and that is certainly true, but it is only part of the story. Over the last several decades failing companies have clawed back their employees' pension funds leaving them with only Social Security to survive on. It is robbery. Congress and the financial industry are guilty of the same crime, the financial industry by not paying us for the use of our money and Congress for transferring our Social Security funds to the general fund and spending it. They might argue that they replaced the money with government bonds that will earn interest. It's a lie. With the government running huge budget deficits, the only place the interest can come from is next years' Social Security premiums. Each year less money is available for benefits. Last year they announced that we would get a 2% increase in benefits, but they raised the Medicare Part D (prescription drug plan) premiums by almost exactly the same amount. Apparently, we had to pay for the huge tax cut for the wealthy.

Once paid in, retirement funds must remain the property of the beneficiary and they must earn interest. It can be accomplished quite easily. The first step is to reinstate an updated Glass Steagall Act to assure our money will be safe. Then commercial banks, especially smaller community banks, will be allowed to contract for some of the money to

RETIREMENT SECURITY

lend out for homes and cars to creditworthy borrowers. Mortgages will be held by the issuing bank until repaid. Each month, the bank will repay the Social Security fund the amount received for principal and a portion of the interest. The Social Security fund and benefit payments will grow to keep pace with inflation. Smaller commercial banks will thrive and we will be less dependent on the largest. The mortgage market will be stabilized. Banks will value their depositors and borrowers. It would be a public/private partnership, so it should not get labeled as socialist.

Social Security is an insurance program, not welfare. We all pay for auto insurance on our cars. Some pay a bit more than others, but everyone pays, even though some might never have an accident. It protects us from catastrophic loss. We pay on the basis of the value of the car. The driver of a Lincoln cannot get insurance on the basis of a Ford Focus. In the case of Social Security, a person's income equates with the value of a car. Why is there a limit on how much income gets charged Social Security premiums? The system can be greatly simplified by paying benefits out of the trust fund and collecting the premiums as part of our income tax payments under the proposed Gross Revenues Tax. Because the beneficiaries spend their benefits almost entirely in privately owned businesses, it supports the free enterprise system and is therefore not socialism.

Most of us get a free ride through early life on the backs of our parents. They provide the necessities of life, education, and protection to their kids, currently often into their thirties. We have a moral obligation to repay their toil when they are no longer able to work or lack the resources to care for themselves. In some Asian societies, extended families live together. The grandparents who can no longer work care for the children and help around the house until they are no longer able to do so. Even then, they are respected, honored, and cared for. Sadly, our me-centered society with its serial divorces has broken those familial bonds. A child may have multiple step-parents and many step-grandparents. That makes the Asian model impracticable here.

Most seniors cannot afford nursing homes or even assisted living or independent living facilities, the least expensive of which cost at least $30,000 per year. **Perhaps if we offered an incentive of one-third of that amount to those willing to take in their parents or family friends, we could provide proper care for less than what we spend on Medicaid.**

RETIREMENT SECURITY

My parents have been gone for many years. They were able to live out their last few years with dignity because of the safety net Social Security provided. They were both hard working and extremely frugal. They did not own a home until the last decade of their lives, and it was little more than a shack, but it brought them great joy. They never owned a car, took only brief vacations to visit family, never attended entertainment events, and never had a credit card. Dad received a small pension of about $100 per month. They never bought anything they could not afford, and saved every penny they could. They were fortunate to live out their working lives in Chicago which had a very good public transportation system and essential services. Employer-provided health insurance covered most of their health care cost until they became eligible for Medicare.

We have been conditioned to believe that there have to be winners and losers, but that only has to be true in games. In real life, we should all have the opportunity to be winners in varying degrees. My parents got along fine without luxuries and the latest toys, cars, credit cards, cable TV, restaurant dining, etc. Their frugality allowed them to live out their retirement in dignity and free of debt, but they could not have done it without Social Security and Medicare.

Their lack of wants and must-haves made them winners to me. They refused to let the financial system entrap them.

The question isn't at what age I want to retire, it's at what income.

George Foreman

HEALTH CARE

The United States have the best medical schools, the best trained doctors, excellent nurses, the best hospitals, the largest number of health care facilities, the most sophisticated medical equipment and more of it, shorter waiting times for many procedures, higher survival rates from many diseases, and spends more by half on health care per capita than any other country. By any measure, it ought to have the healthiest people in the world. Why doesn't it?

Most of the industrial nations on earth have universal health care plans, many of which are single payer systems administered by their governments. The world's highest level of satisfaction with their health care system is in France, which spends less than half per person than we do. Japan spends the least among the nations I studied yet it has the longest life expectancy and second lowest infant mortality rate. We, who spend by far the most, have some of the highest rates of obesity, diabetes, heart disease, cancer, and other ailments. There is an obvious disconnect between the cost of our health care and the results. The debate about health care reform has become so highly politicized that it is virtually impossible to determine what the facts are and what reforms would bring down cost and improve results.

No doubt some of the differences are due to lifestyle. We are less physically active, eat more highly processed foods laden with preservatives, and consume tremendous quantities of sugars, sodas, and cheeses. Many of us live on a deep fried fast food diet devoid of fruits and vegetables. Our refrigerators are huge by comparison to those in other countries. Most foreign families shop each day for fresh meats, breads, fruits, and vegetables. They eat a broader variety of foods, which provide more of the essential nutrients. We have sacrificed quality for convenience. Our Food and Drug Administration has not adequately regulated and enforced food quality standards. We need a radical reeducation on nutrition and its effect on health, but that is beyond the scope of this chapter.

Our health care system is in crisis, both in cost and quality of outcomes. Members of Congress speak of the health care crisis, but most are unwilling to face the wrath of the special interests to do something about it. With health insurance premiums averaging nearly the entire income of a minimum wage worker, very few

HEALTH CARE

businesses can afford health insurance for their employees, so they are either reducing their share of health insurance premiums or dropping health insurance entirely. Many employers are hiring part time workers only to avoid providing health care benefits. Employer provided health care is a major factor in making our businesses noncompetitive in a global economy.

We do not have a health care system. We have several, including two socialist health care systems: government owned and staffed Veterans Administration and military hospitals in military bases. Tri-Care provides health insurance coverage for active duty and retired military personnel and their families largely at taxpayer expense. Medicare provides health care coverage for seniors and disabled persons. Medicaid, which provides healthcare coverage for the poor, is actually fifty systems since each state administers its own. Health Maintenance Organizations (HMOs) provide coverage to their members through health care providers who are members of their network. Because Medicare, Medicaid, and Tri-Care negotiate prices many doctors refuse to accept their patients. All of these systems have their own administrations. The administrative cost at most private insurers is nine times that at Medicare, the Canadian health system, and many other single payer systems. Much of our administrative cost goes into denying coverage rather than providing care. Combining these systems into one comprehensive single payer health care system would save at least 15% and billions of dollars in administrative cost alone.

Prescription drug costs are a major component of our health care cost. We have all heard about the maker of the Epi-Pen raising the price 600% to $600. It is a product that costs less than $7 to manufacture. It is a life saver carried by many people with various allergies who can lapse into anaphylactic shock and die if not treated immediately. The market for it is huge as is the profit potential at the original price of $100. This outrageous behavior has reached the level of insanity. It is only possible because the pharmaceutical industry has formed a union of sorts to fix prices and stifle competition. I use a drop of lubricating eye ointment every night to relieve dry eyes. Two years ago a tube of Muro 128 cost $9. Now it costs $26. It is petroleum jelly with 5% saline in a one-eighth ounce tube, the cost of which cannot exceed $1. Pharmaceutical industry top executives are thieves and Congress is complicit in their crimes. It is Congress that prevented Medicare from negotiating drug prices and preventing us from buying our drugs from international sources.

HEALTH CARE

Competition is the cornerstone of capitalism. It is not capitalism to prevent competition or bribe doctors to prescribe the costliest drugs. Insurance companies don't care about our health care costs because they are cost plus businesses.

Pharmaceutical companies spend far more on marketing and advertizing their products than on research and development of new drugs. I cannot buy a prescription drug without my doctor's prescription. Why are we one of the only countries that allow pharmaceutical companies to advertise directly to consumers? It is an unwarranted expense that comes out of our pockets. Kickbacks to doctors who prescribe their products should also be illegal. I pay the doctor for his services. The pharmaceutical industry and Congress are also responsible for the current opioid epidemic that is displacing illegal drug cartels as suppliers of choice for addicts.

Why are so many of us becoming addicted? We recognize that military personnel experience extreme battlefield stress and suffer post traumatic stress disorder (PTSD) for years after. Why can we not recognize the financial, educational, workplace, family and social stresses that so many suffer from? For many, alcohol, drugs, and marijuana bring momentary relief, but at the cost of long term disability. Our emphasis has been on physical health, but we have mostly ignored mental health as treatable disease. We need to learn from other countries that have effective programs to deal with this issue.

Another major driver of health care cost is medical malpractice insurance. Just last month I read that someone had been awarded $167 million in a medical malpractice lawsuit. The amount is outrageous. We are bombarded with TV advertising by personal injury law firms bragging up their ability to get money for us. I have some sympathy for the injured wanting to sue because both my mother and my wife's mother died because of doctors' errors. We did not sue the doctors because we recognize that they make mistakes like all the rest of us and we did not want to profit from our mothers' misfortunes. However there must be a deterrent to negligence and therefore the right to sue. The challenge is to set up a system that provides necessary tort reform without damaging the health care system. Consider this proposal:

In a serious criminal case, the case is presented to a grand jury which decides whether the case should go to trial, whether the charges are applicable, and what limits might be necessary on the prosecution. **We should create a civil grand jury system to evaluate lawsuits**

HEALTH CARE

to determine if the lawsuit is justified, whether it is timely, what the extent of economic damage is, how much pain and suffering is involved, the extent of negligence or harmful intent, any limits on awards, and whether the case should proceed to trial. Small claims cases would not merit civil grand jury evaluation. Eliminating frivolous lawsuits and limiting awards to a reasonable level would significantly reduce medical malpractice insurance cost and overall health care cost.

All we have left to do is **set up the single payer system, a hybrid of Medicare and Tricare that would cover 100% of the cost for all covered situations**. Private insurers would cover all other types of casualty, liability, and business insurance. The system would involve a central administrative entity. For the sake of convenience, let's call it CHAP, the Central Health Administration Partnership. **There would be no need for Medicare, Medicaid, and VA, all with their own administrative functions.** Military hospitals and clinics would only serve active duty military personnel and their families, although, if the military system were completely compatible with the civilian system, there would be no reason why they could not receive their care wherever they want. **All participants, military and civilian, would enjoy complete portability**

of their coverage, including while traveling in foreign countries. CHAP would negotiate prices with global pharmaceutical companies and qualified providers to keep prices in check and to force domestic companies and foreign competitors to develop the most effective advanced treatments.

One change that has great potential for reducing cost and improving quality is the **creation of a central health care database** in each state or region and backed up at the national level. It would contain all insurance information, privacy preferences, living will statements, medical history, prescription data, identify all providers, and record all treatments and related costs. It would eliminate the need for paper records at the provider's facility and reduce the need for providers to negotiate with insurance companies. Medical histories would be more accurate and would not have to be recreated for each provider. With the records securely encrypted, privacy concerns should be minimal.

Imagine walking into your doctor's office, scanning your positive identification card (PID), and having your complete medical record available to him on his laptop computer. At the end of your visit, your record would be updated with any new findings and instructions,

HEALTH CARE

prescription changes, referrals, etc. Any laboratory results and MRI, CT, and other images would also be available during your visit. With today's peer-to-peer relational database technology and data mining capability, a fully redundant secure system is possible. Upon scanning the PID smart card, your photo and other personal identifying information would download to the doctor's laptop, your pharmacy's computer, or anywhere else where you would need to positively identify yourself.

There are many advantages to such a system. Identity theft becomes extremely difficult. Medical mistakes should occur much less frequently. Any allergies you have would be immediately known to all providers. Hospitals would not have to determine what your wishes are in the event you are unable to communicate them. Statistical analyses of the database would make fraud easier to spot, aid in determining the effectiveness of treatments, and identify possible drug interactions and side effects. Complete medical cost data would be available on a timely basis. It would also make it easier to identify those addicted to prescription drugs and those prescribing them. It would also help to identify incompetent providers.

The right to life must by extension also be the right to comprehensive health care. I tried to keep health insurance companies as an integral part of the health care system, but found that it complicated the system to an unacceptable degree. It would be a return to something like the Affordable Care Act (Obamacare) that was unable to lower health care cost partly because of insurance company and political opposition. Ask me how we could fund such an expansion of health care.

A portion of tax receipts would be placed in a health insurance trust fund (HIT) similar to the Social Security trust fund proposed in the chapter on *Retirement Security.* It would also be contracted out to commercial banks to be lent out to creditworthy borrowers and repaid to HIT with interest. Under no circumstances would Congress ever be able to transfer any part of it for any other purpose. The fund would therefore always keep pace with inflation. It would not be socialism because hospitals and other health care providers would continue to be privately owned.

I, who do not believe in socialized health-care, would advocate a single-payment system... because it will get this monster that we've created out of the economy and allow the rest of capitalism to flourish without the awful things that healthcare is doing to us. Angus Deaton

IMMIGRATION

Illegal immigration has been put forth as a problem primarily on our southern border. That is a gross oversimplification. The truth is that tens of millions of people enter this country legally on tourist, student, and work visas from nations all over the world by air, sea, and land. Many simply overstay their visas, and we have no effective system in place to identify, track, and remove them. Furthermore, citizens of more than two-dozen countries do not even need a visa to enter the United States. Several of the 9/11 highjackers came here legally. If we are serious about the war on terror, then solving this problem is every bit as important as securing our borders. An effective solution has to deal with all sources of illegal immigration.

Illegal immigration increases our unemployment rate and stresses our health care and education budgets. The Latinos that cross our borders illegally are mostly from Central and South American countries, some of which are horrifically violent places. They come here looking for a better and safer life. Our love of cheap products and our businesses' love of cheap labor keeps them coming. The same politicians who inflame anti-immigrant sentiment refuse to put any constraints on businesses that hire illegal aliens. Whatever immigration laws have been proposed or passed have less to do with stopping illegal immigration than they do about making it a hot button political issue.

Building a wall on our southern border borders on insanity. It does nothing to address the causes of illegal immigration: failures in political, economic, and criminal justice systems in neighboring countries and availability of jobs here. A wall in densely populated urban border areas might help, but that would only include a small fraction of the border. Elsewhere it would only waste money. All it takes to defeat a tall fence is a tall ladder or deep tunnel. The Israelis built an enormous border wall to keep Palestinians out. It did not prevent them from tunneling under the wall to attack Israelis. Drug traffickers have tunneled under the wall at San Diego. Desperate people will do whatever it takes to provide for their families. Whether they are refugees escaping violence in their own countries or economic migrants, they would not come here if the supply of jobs was cut off.

The notion that illegal immigrants only take jobs Americans won't do is false. In my previous life as a senior executive in an international manufacturing company, our U.S. factories employed workers at relatively low pay. The workforce consisted of about one-third each African-Americans, Hispanics, and whites. Some of the whites were Polish immigrants here on two-year work visas or legal permanent residents. The Hispanics all had social security numbers, but on several occasions, more than one or two people had the same number. Although we never intentionally hired illegal immigrants, there is little doubt that some were. The jobs were difficult, fast paced factory work. An incentive system allowed workers to earn more by exceeding productivity standards. We never had any difficulty finding legal workers willing to do the jobs. Once properly trained, all three groups performed equally well. If a company provides proper training, supervision, discipline, and sound management, it will find legal workers willing to do most jobs. The lone exception may be the work performed by migratory farm workers conditioned to work stooped over picking fruits and vegetables in intense heat for hours, which few Americans are fit to do.

I love this country. I am a legal immigrant and United States citizen. In my earliest years, my family and I experienced the brutal Soviet occupation of Eastern Poland, then barely survived two Nazi concentration camps, and endured four years in refugee camps. Our experiences gave us a different perspective than many Americans who tend to mythologize history. Let me share a few insights into the immigrant experience with you.

Most immigrants that arrived in the United States were indeed grateful. My family and I certainly were. America had helped free us from slavery under the Nazis. We entered the U.S. not at Ellis Island but New Orleans. Our first place of residence in the United States was in Perry County, Arkansas, the poorest county in all of the United States at that time. Fortunately for us, the surrounding community had many German-speaking people. My parents and siblings spoke German well. I spoke little German. The only way I could communicate with my teachers and classmates was to learn English.

For the first six months, we worked without pay, except for room and board. We lived in a one-room log cabin with dirt floor. Most of our meals consisted of sweet potatoes and buttermilk. A compassionate doctor, himself a Polish immigrant who immigrated to the U.S. back in the 1920s, helped us to break away from our sponsor. We rented a shack without electricity, gas, or running water, for $5 per month. It was on about four acres of land. Before we were able to grow any vegetables, we went without food for up to four days at a time. Kind neighbors, seeing our plight, reached out to help us. The pastor of our little church came with a twenty-five pound sack of flour. A neighbor brought some milk and eggs. By the end of summer, we were self-sufficient. When my father found a job, he was paid 27 cents an hour, half the minimum wage at the time. It took three years to save enough money for one train ticket out of Arkansas. When my dad arrived in Chicago, he slept on the floor in an apartment shared with two other families. Without the support of the community, we would have starved. Any success I have enjoyed since then is due in large measure to the welfare provided by the United Nations Relief Agency, Catholic Relief Services, our church, and good neighbors. God bless them all! A hand up is not a handout.

Learning English was never a major consideration—survival was. Cities like New York, Chicago, Minneapolis, San Francisco, and others had schools that taught in Italian, Polish, German, Norwegian, Chinese and other languages until sometime after World War II. Ethnic communities within these cities provided a support structure well into the second and third generation. The children were usually the first to learn English. The parents learned only enough to get by in the workplace. Most adults could not afford to go to school to learn English. They were usually underpaid and worked long hours, often without a day off.

When we finally got to Chicago, my parents were grateful to be in a Polish neighborhood where they could have a relatively normal life. Most stores in our neighborhood had Polish-speaking help. Most places of employment had someone who could interpret. Our church had a service in Polish. Italian and German neighborhoods provided similar support to their residents. My parents learned English slowly, as do most adults, because the workplace made it necessary, especially when immigrants began to leave their ethnic communities in search of better opportunities. Their lack of English language skills in no way impaired their love for the United States of America. We should all be proud of our ethnic heritage, as well as being proud of being Americans. There is some beauty and value in every culture.

English is and will continue to be the dominant language of the United States. There is no need to make it the official language by law, which would prohibit any dual-language official documents. Doing so only serves to increase the difficulty for all immigrants, including those here legally. The company I worked for had operations in Canada, England, and Germany, an office in Hong Kong, customers and suppliers in nearly sixty countries. In Canada, our product packaging, warranties, and other literature were printed in three languages: French-Canadian, English, and Spanish. It would not have made sense to try to sell our products to the large French-speaking consumer base if they could not read our product information. The same is true of Hispanics and other large consumer groups in the US.

There is nothing wonderful about the hardships we endured and nothing bad about multilingual societies. Illegal immigration is a serious problem that needs to be solved, but it cannot be solved by the methods proposed to date. As long as businesses can hire illegal aliens with impunity, and we have no means of knowing who they are, they will continue to come, regardless of how tall the walls we build, whether we mandate English as the only official language, deny them education or health care, or deport them. Most of us would do exactly what they do if we lived under the same conditions they escaped from.

The choice is ours. We can continue the course we are on — keep cutting taxes for corporations and the rich, exporting good paying jobs, importing cheap labor, and increasing the national debt — all the while pretending we are defending our borders by detaining and deporting those crossing them illegally. That will ultimately make our economy just like that of the countries illegal immigrants came here to escape. They will have no reason to come here. The alternative is to enact real immigration reforms.

Before we can control illegal immigration, we must have some means of determining who the illegal immigrants and other aliens are. The time has come for a secure tamperproof positive identification card that contains a person's encrypted name and aliases, DNA, fingerprint, biometric, immigration status, citizenship, and place of origin data plus digital photo as well as a visible one, and a unique encryption key. The identifying data should be maintained on secure encrypted databases with restricted access. It may seem somewhat burdensome, but it will have benefits in many other areas such as prevention of terrorism, identity theft, Medicare fraud, and crime in general. Ultimately, the card could serve as a drivers' license, credit card, electronic signature, proof of insurance, medical authorization, professional certification, firearms carry permit, and a myriad of other uses. Identity theft would become extremely difficult.

Imagine a card reader capable of displaying a photo and other needed information at immigration points, transportation ticket counters, wherever cell phones and other communication devices are sold, hospitals and doctors' offices, police stations, gun shops, currency exchanges, and banks. The cards should be interactive so that they can be updated automatically to include new data when they are used. Scanning the card should display the decrypted photo, name and address, telephone numbers, immigration status, and other data critical for the type of transaction being processed. The benefits to citizens would far outweigh any privacy concerns, especially since all critical data would always remain encrypted. We could issue an identity card to every arriving alien, and document their arrivals and departures. The database would maintain a record of their whereabouts, and notify authorities of overstays. Passports can be forged. The identity card cannot, and so can act as a passport as well. The database could be screened to find people with multiple identities. Stealing a card would do the thief no good because the thief's appearance and other characteristics would not match.

Let me put any privacy concerns you have to rest. If you are not an illegal alien, you have no privacy. For a few dollars, anyone can access your unlisted phone number, every address you have had, what schools you attended, your criminal record, known associates and relatives, credit history, social security number, what you read, what television programs you watch, where you eat, what your hobbies are, and much more. Insurance companies, credit card companies, cable companies, and many others maintain databases of this information. Most of it is available to affiliated firms, marketers, and anyone else willing to pay for it. Why do you think you get travel brochures after you research cruise lines on the Internet, or magazine subscription offers of interest to you? The politicians yielded to the special interests in this regard also. You should not have to opt out of anyone's privacy policy to keep your personal information confidential.

Student visas have been an area of concern for national security. Universities should be required to report aliens on student visas that drop out without reapplying in another school, in which case their visas should be revoked.

Once a positive identification system is in place, we should require every alien to register within six months, or leave the country. They will not register unless there is an incentive to do so. A promise that they will not be deported if they have not committed a serious crime, that those who have not registered will lose their jobs and be deported, and that their employers and

IMMIGRATION

customers will face prosecution for hiring unregistered aliens should help them decide to register.

To ease the initial implementation burden, legal permanent resident aliens and citizens could be processed after the six month period. Aliens who have not committed a serious felony should be allowed to remain in the United States and be granted permanent resident status. While this is amnesty of sorts, it will dramatically reduce the number of illegal aliens entering the country in the future. It is also the humane and reasonable thing to do. Legal migratory workers should be required to leave the country after each planting and harvest season.

The next step, to be taken within the first twelve months, should be to **require all employers to certify that all their employees are registered**. All corporate officers and business owners, as well as the Human Resources Manager, should sign the certification. **Thereafter, we should imprison the employers' Chief Executive Officer (or owner), Human Resources Manager, and any other manager or person who hires an alien without the proper identification**. Monetary penalties for employers do not work. They are often far less than the savings from employing illegal aliens.

Thereafter we should immediately deport any unregistered aliens with their immediate families. Arrest and deportation orders for aliens who violate their visas or commit felonies should be issued automatically. Any deported alien who returns to this country illegally should be imprisoned for a mandatory minimum sentence of two years, and then deported again.

No legal immigrants should be allowed into the country if the unemployment rate exceeds 4%, with the possible exception of a few political refugees and migrant farm workers. The current method of determining the unemployment rate is a farce. It does not account for undocumented work, partial employment, and the discouraged that have quit looking. We should require US employers to report their employment as part of their monthly GRT tax return. It should include all information needed for accurate employment statistics.

. Once this proposal is implemented and enforced, only the criminals and terrorists will have a reason to risk crossing our borders. Manpower and technology are the best ways to deal with those threats. Immigration and customs officials and their superiors must comply with all applicable laws or face termination, imprisonment, or impeachment.

IMMIGRATION

Let's let our politicians know that they work for us, not drug cartels and big business.

We must change the law on citizenship by birth. If a terrorist's favorite daughter has a child born while visiting the United States, should that child be a United States citizen? Absolutely not!. **A child born in the United States should be a citizen only if at least one parent is a citizen, or both parents are legal permanent residents.**

We can solve the illegal immigration problem, but we should do so with common sense and compassion.

Remember, remember always, that all of us, and you and I especially, are descended from immigrations and revolutionists.

Franklin D. Roosevelt (1882-1945), President of the United States

Learning and innovation go hand in hand. The arrogance of success is to think that what you did yesterday will be sufficient for tomorrow.

William Pollard

NO CHILD LEFT BEHIND

The United States has some of the best universities in the world. Citizens of foreign countries strive to have their children educated here. Nonetheless, we are losing our technological edge. Why is that? A fitting analogy may be a computer – the quality of the output cannot be better than the input. The problem is not at the university level; it is at the elementary level. You have undoubtedly heard some of the reasons: unqualified teachers, tenure, large class sizes, insufficient classroom hours, social promotion, inadequate testing, unrecognized learning disabilities, underfunding, powerful teachers' unions, etc. These may be contributing factors, but I don't believe most of them are causative. I am not an expert in the field of education, but I believe you will find my observations and suggestions to be correct.

My education began in a United Nations refugee camp in Germany after World War II. By the end of first grade, every Polish child in my class could read everything it was given. I am not implying that each child necessarily understood everything it read, but it could read and pronounce the words correctly. There was no social promotion and no teachers' union, but all the other factors cited above were present. So why does it take children here four or more years to learn to read reasonably well?

Most of my formative years were spent before recorded music, radio, television, movies, computers, computer games, telephones, and social media filled our heads with trivialities. All those things that have eased our lives and entertained us have also placed an inordinate demand on our memory capacity, and have reduced our attention spans. At the same time, there has been a tremendous explosion of knowledge in nearly every field, so there is much more that needs to be learned.

Studies of child prodigies have shown that a child's level of achievement in a given discipline is based upon the level of interest in it and is often proportional to the level of parental commitment. Child prodigies tend to learn by total immersion. That can become a full time job for a parent. There is a difference between a prodigy, who develops an exceptional skill in one field, and a genius, who has extraordinary intelligence and ability in a broad range of subjects. The study habits formed this way often make it possible for prodigies to change interests and become high achievers in a new field. The key word is interests. Children rarely become proficient in subjects they find uninteresting or monotonous, or those that are so challenging that they can never experience some success.

We must shift our focus from teaching classes a fixed curriculum of subjects to make student well-rounded to teaching individual students those subjects they are interested in and for which they have an aptitude. Each student's education should be coordinated between the various classes. For example, if a student has interest in some period in history, reading that material would be far more rewarding than reading Shakespeare or Dickens. For another student, reading about some aspect of science or engineering would be more beneficial than the works of modern novelists. The same should apply to mathematics. The math taught to the student should be geared to the direction of the student's interest and ability. That makes it a lot tougher for the teachers, but it helps to develop expertise in areas that have occupational potential. Most people develop their own tastes in music, art, and literature. It is certainly helpful for a student to learn how to do basic sketching for the purpose of communicating ideas graphically, but knowing what style Van Gogh painted in or how he lost an ear is only useful to the student who chooses art education as a career. I am very much in favor of a cafeteria system where a child can take short introductory courses early on to determine the child's aptitudes and interests.

Boredom and monotony destroy the desire for learning. Not every child learns the same way. One child can absorb information it hears, another gets more out of graphic presentations, yet another can process what is read, and some get the most out of hands-on projects. The most effective teachers use lectures, reading assignments, videos, and hands-on team projects. The brightest students are the ones most likely to become bored. They must be allowed to advance beyond their grade level on a subject by subject basis. Relatively inexpensive tablet computers can give them access to many online educational resources.

Learning takes time. As this was being written a news program announced that nearly half of the schools in our area had gone to a four day week. Some schools have gone to half day classes. Students and teachers alike love having more free time, but they will pay a high price for that time. It will give unsupervised children even more time without parental supervision and less time for learning. Just because students and teachers feel good about it does not mean that it is good for them. We are already paying for our

NO CHILD LEFT BEHIND

schools and our children's education. We should take maximum advantage of that infrastructure to provide more time for learning, less unsupervised time for children, and reduce the crushing cost of day care.

When we were an agrarian society and there was no air conditioning, taking three months off during the summer made sense. Children could help on the farm during extended daylight hours and avoid stifling hot classrooms. Today, we have air conditioning, family farms are fewer, and modern farms and farm machinery have their own illumination. With both parents working, the child is either unsupervised for long periods of time or the parents are stuck with three consecutive months of daycare expense. Lack of supervision often provides an opportunity for kids to get into trouble. Some of what was learned before the summer break must be relearned. A better plan, in my opinion, is to spread the time off over the year, perhaps four eleven-week quarters with one week off each in the spring and fall, two during the winter holidays, and a four week vacation period in the summer. This allows children to participate in fun activities in each season of the year, adds four weeks of education, and lessens the risk of burnout.

None of this would make day care centers unnecessary. Working mothers with toddlers would still need them. School districts could alternate spring, fall, winter and summer break times between schools to keep day care centers filled most of the time.

I propose that our schools provide all-day preschool for children from the age of three. Their days should include lunch and break times, early learning (reading, writing, math, music, art), team activities, nap time and rest periods, games, and sports. It would not be necessary for one teacher to be present for a child's entire day if we overlap teachers' schedules. A variety of subjects and activities would prevent boredom and stimulate the desire to learn. A similar approach in higher class levels should provide the same benefits.

Few parents today have the luxury of a stay-at-home spouse. My parents both had to work to survive. A single parent often has no choice but to work multiple jobs. The absence of parents due to divorce, multiple jobs, and irresponsible lifestyles, means that children must fend for themselves much of the time. Sometimes a family member can provide childcare, but most often it is entrusted to a childcare center or other non-family care giver who cannot give the individualized attention needed for proper

NO CHILD LEFT BEHIND

development of reasoning and memory. When the child outgrows the need for a childcare center, it is left without supervision of any sort for a significant part of its day. This is not a formula for success.

One study I read stated that about ten percent of elementary school students have been diagnosed with attention deficit/hyperactivity disorder (ADHD), and two-thirds of them are being medicated. It seems to help, but who is it helping -- the teacher, the parent, or the child? And, what effect is it having on their academic performance? I believe that hyperactivity is not a congenital condition but one that develops as a byproduct of parental failure to exercise their parental authority. These days, bedtimes and study times are rarely enforced. Meals are often taken on the fly, or in front of the television, making it difficult for a family to communicate. That, in turn, leads to alienation. Children invariably do their homework in front of the television or listening to music. The parents allow it because it is easier to give in than fight. They are rarely required to do chores or clean up messes they create. Since they are never corrected, they do not develop coping skills, ability to follow schedules or organize its activities or spaces. When demands are placed on them, they become, frustrated, bewildered, depressed, rebellious, anti-social, or even suicidal.

Another factor that may affect the quality of our education is the overemphasis on sports. Parents may push their children into sports in hopes of them earning college scholarships on the basis of athletic ability, overlooking the fact that only a tiny fraction of college students ever goes on to make a living in sports. This would not pose a problem if it did not relegate academics to a lower priority. What does it say about our priorities when a high school coach is paid much more than the school principal?

Home study and homework can be a real problem for the one-third of high school students who also work, some to 10:00 or 11:00 PM. The choice becomes homework and study or sleep. You can guess which often wins out. Sports and other extracurricular activities also squeeze the time available for schoolwork. Even when sufficient time is available, there are just too many distractions in the home. It would make far more sense to revise our class schedules to permit study and homework in a longer class without cell phones, iPods, and gaming devices. Study, discussion, and homework would all be done while the teacher is available to answer any questions, memories are fresh, and there are no distractions. It would also give teachers

NO CHILD LEFT BEHIND

sufficient time in class to grade papers and do lesson plans. The most demanding subjects should be taught early in the day when minds are fresh. Allowing a longer lunch and break periods would minimize students' need to leave class for restroom breaks, and give children and teachers a needed break. That makes for a longer school day with eight classes, but it comes with two additional benefits: reduced daycare costs and less unsupervised after-school time for children.

Adding time alone will not improve the quality of education. Most discussions of the subject eventually get around to firing bad teachers. There is a near consensus that it is very difficult to get rid of bad teachers because of teachers unions, and that getting rid of them would improve education. There are a number of problems with this premise. How can we tell who the bad teachers are? Were they always bad, or were they somehow made bad by the system? Does money somehow figure in the equation?

A few years ago, the chancellor of Washington, D.C. public schools, which spent more than $15,000 a year per student, fired nearly 100 of the central office staff, two dozen principals, almost that many assistant principals, approximately 260 teachers, and nearly twice that many teaching aides. She closed more than twenty schools and reorganized more than two dozen others. She also renegotiated the contract with the teachers union that would give them the option to give up seniority pay for a chance at much higher merit pay. Graduation rate increased three percent. Reading and math scores came up a bit, and writing skills improved somewhat. If replacing teachers alone was the solution, the D.C. schools should have shown much more significant results.

Two of our children attended parochial schools. When we moved to an upscale community with a public school reputed to be one of the very best in the country, we decided to enroll our children there. Within two months, our children were terribly bored. They were studying material they had learned in the parochial school eighteen months earlier. We had no choice but to put them back in the more distant parochial school. Parents of the public school children felt their children were getting an excellent education, and that the teachers were doing a good job. Their teachers were getting paid more than those in the parochial school. They had better facilities and larger budgets. What conclusions can we draw from that experience? I can think of several:

- We do not have effective ways of evaluating schools or teachers.

NO CHILD LEFT BEHIND

- Money alone does not guarantee good education.
- School choice is a good thing.
- More structured and disciplined environments are more conducive to learning.

Programs set up to weed out inadequate teachers and close underperforming schools spawned a wave of cheating scandals in Chicago, Atlanta, and Pennsylvania, with teachers changing students' test scores to make themselves look better. Texas, an early adopter of a similar testing program had the second highest high school dropout rate in the country. Schools have found that pushing poor students out is every bit as effective at raising scores as educating them, and it is easier than getting rid of poor teachers. One news report pointed out that once alternative schooling has been recommended for a student, that student is removed from the rolls, thereby raising the schools performance numbers. Black and Hispanic students have by far the highest rate of high school dropouts. Not coincidentally, they also come from the poorest families.

It is difficult for a parent to know how good a school is or whether their child is performing satisfactorily. Report cards do not tell the whole story. The proliferation of privately operated charter, magnet, alternative, and church affiliated schools provides choices, but how are we to know that they are any better than the public schools? They should be subject to the same testing process with the same safeguards. Teachers should not be the ones to administer tests used to determine their own effectiveness. Teachers should also be tested periodically to determine their knowledge of the subject(s) they teach. That testing should take place at a different facility and be administered by someone outside of their district and administration.

Their students should be tested similarly. Any one test can be misleading, so testing should be done frequently, perhaps semiannually, with each succeeding test somewhat more difficult. The exact test to be used should be a surprise to all parties concerned, being selected at random at the last moment. There should be enough different tests that teaching to a particular test or cheating would be less likely. Results should not be based on grade levels, which are a moving target, but on absolute percentage scores. Each question or problem should have a percentage of difficulty assigned. The test should be graded by the average difficulty ratings of the questions answered correctly and the percentage of all questions that were answered correctly. Ideally, both figures should be recorded because they would more readily identify students' developmental problems.

With all the testing and grading a teacher must do, it suggests we should automate part of that process. Tests and homework could be formatted to be scanned and graded by computer using a scanner similar to that used by polling places during elections. Students should also be able to do homework and take tests on their tablet computers and submit them electronically.

After the third or fourth grade, teachers should specialize in the subjects they teach. Students should be able to jump grades on a subject by subject basis so they can continue to be challenged and advance most in the subjects in which they show the greatest interest and ability. That means classes should be set up to teach specific subjects with all the necessary equipment and supplies present. Moving from class to class would provide changes of scenery and reduce boredom.

The high cost of higher education may be partly responsible for the astounding high-school dropout rate. It is certainly beyond the reach of most families. College tuitions and student loan interest rates have soared without a commensurate increase in salaries of college graduates. The average college debt now exceeds $37,000, near what a graduate with a bachelor's degree can earn in a year. The uncertainty of later employment, staggering cost, and fear of indebtedness may scare off many high school students from pursuing higher education. Student loans are not relieved under bankruptcy. The export of quality jobs makes repayment of student loans problematic.

Firing people and closing underperforming schools is easy. The same students and teachers then go to other schools, and drag down their performance. Teachers should be tested for knowledge of the subjects they teach and their teaching skills, only be allowed to teach subjects in which they can meet certain minimal standards, and be required to either teach a lower grade for which the teacher can meet the standard or take remedial classes if there is a likelihood of meeting a standard. It is difficult, in terms of time and finances, for a teacher with a family to work and take classes. We should be willing to pay the teacher's salary for a few weeks while taking the classes. Failure to meet the standards after taking the classes would justify termination. There is no guarantee that replacement teachers will perform any better. Smart college graduates can earn far more in other professions than in teaching. If we want qualified teachers we must pay them what they are worth. How do we determine what they are worth?

Some have argued that teachers should be paid based on merit. This assumes that once a teacher has achieved proficiency they will remain proficient. That is not necessarily the case. I have had a number of outstanding employees who received repeated merit salary increases, but could not sustain that high level of performance, and were ultimately priced out of the market. Performance evaluations tend to be subjective, and vary broadly from manager to manager. They are rarely free of bias. The amount of education a person has received is also not a certain indicator of performance. I believe teacher compensation should be based on the difficulty of the subject taught, the amount of education required to achieve and maintain mastery, and the performance of their students compared to others in the same demographic based on impartial testing.

Primary and secondary education is funded largely by community-based property taxes. You may have heard it said that 'money does not guarantee good education'. That may be true, but why are the best schools typically found in affluent communities? Inequitable distribution of education funding affects class size, teacher compensation, ability to attract qualified teachers, and availability of the best materials and programs. The College Board, a non-profit organization that administers Scholastic Achievement Tests, has published figures showing that students from the wealthiest homes score the highest, while those from the poorest homes score the lowest. Property taxes are an anachronism. I believe two-thirds of all primary and secondary education should be paid for from the general fund based on the gross revenues tax on individuals and corporations in the nation. The remaining one-third should be based on the gross revenues tax collected from the postal code(s) in each school district. That would still allow wealthier communities to spend more per pupil, but would level the playing field somewhat.

Parents of private or parochial school students pay twice for their children's education, once in their taxes, and then in tuition. In many cases, these schools provide a better education at lower cost. Would we not be better off to put some of our tax money to work there? I do not believe that the separation of church and state clause of our Constitution, which prohibits the establishment of a state religion, would be violated if all religious and secular schools were

NO CHILD LEFT BEHIND

treated equally if they met performance standards. Our founding fathers encouraged religious education.

In listening to the wrangling over the sad state of our educational system, I am appalled at the lack of any creative solutions in the proposals. I am generally in favor of a longer school day and school year, and I believe incompetent teachers should be dismissed after remedial efforts have failed. However, if such a large number of teachers need to be fired, the problem is greater than the teachers. It is the management and the system. For example, the labor contracts negotiated with teachers' unions were negotiated by managements of school districts. The defined benefit retirement plans that were negotiated are nearly impossible to fund, and make education unaffordable when they are funded. The resulting pressure on education budgets forces teachers' salaries down to unacceptable levels considering the amount of education required.

If money alone could cure the problems, then Washington, D.C., should have some of the best schools in the country. If it did indeed spend more than $15,000 per student annually, where was the money going? It was not to teachers' salaries. Teachers in our community often buy school supplies for their classes out of their own pockets because their schools' budgets are so tight. Perhaps the situation in Falcon, a rapidly growing suburb of Colorado Springs, might shed some light on the issue. Many of the students come from the surrounding rural communities. A few years ago, it was reported that they were debating how to cope with budget cuts due to declining revenues from the state. Among the proposed cuts were eliminating student bus service and lunch programs on which nineteen percent of the students depended. In addition, the school board decided to terminate the contracts of their school district's administrative staff as part of an initiative to move decision making lower down the organization structure to principals. According to the *Colorado Springs Gazette* and several other sources, the staff reductions required buyouts of about $1.1 million. They included:

- Chief Financial Officer $260,220
- Director of Human Resources $233,246
- Chief Information Officer $264,004

The Superintendant was to have his title changed to CEO, which would have relegated his role more to educational issues than administrative. Perceiving this as a demotion, he decided to resign instead. His buyout was $225,000. He had been hired eighteen months

NO CHILD LEFT BEHIND

earlier at a salary of $180,000. His prospective successor wanted to match or exceed that figure. This raises a number of questions. Why do we need all these school districts each with their own expensive administrations? What functions do they serve? What do they do to improve quality of education? Would we not be better off with a testing facility for teachers and students in each county?

School districts allow wealthier communities to have better schools because the property tax revenues that support them do not cross district boundaries. They have greater buying power than individual schools, so presumably they should be able to get a better deal. Suppliers love centralized purchasing. Without adequate controls, corruption often creeps in, not just in school systems, but in private businesses and government agencies. When Chicago's former mayor, Richard M. Daley Jr. assumed control of the schools, his management team found warehouses full of rotting food, more than 4,000 desks, almost 9,000 chairs, and nine pianos. The director of facilities was jailed for accepting bribes to funnel projects to favored contractors. Many others were fired for corruption or incompetence. It should surprise no one that the public schools spent twice as much per student annually than

Chicago's highly acclaimed Catholic schools. The business world is no different. I have on more than one occasion fired managers for taking bribes. That is why the purchasing, accounting, and operations functions should never be under common management.

All of the preceding factors have some impact on our children's education. Technological change has increased how much we need to know, while filling our minds with trivia and reducing our capacity for essential knowledge and reasoning ability. Every time I see a spelling bee, I am chagrined at seeing children memorizing words that they will never use. Have you noticed that most of the winners in recent years are Asian? Why is that? I believe it is because of close extended family relationships, more structured and disciplined home environments, and the importance placed on quality education as a key to future success.

Foreigners are generally more adept at learning languages than Americans. Most Americans cannot pronounce foreign words correctly. For example, the Revolutionary War hero, Polish General Kosciuszko, always comes out as either something unrecognizable or 'cozzie-ass-ko'. There is no effective way for me to give you the correct pronunciation in writing because there is no set way to transliterate that

NO CHILD LEFT BEHIND

word into English. The closest I can come is 'cause-chew-sh-ko'. The soft 'sh' should actually be pronounced as 'sz', the sound of frozen chicken in a deep fryer. English is an agglomeration of many languages, each with its own spelling and pronunciation. Without knowing the etymology, or word origin, it is difficult to pronounce the word correctly, except by hearing and memorizing the correct pronunciation, a very memory intensive process.

Children are born with logical minds. They learn quite easily what makes logical sense. If something follows simple straightforward rules, which are applied consistently in similar cases, then it can be learned easily, and it can be remembered easily. Unfortunately, the evolution of language has little to do with logic. Most languages are the product of the mixing of cultures, each with numerous loan words from other languages, and their own spellings and pronunciations. This creates the necessity for memorizing the spelling, pronunciation, and usage of each word, a tragic waste of learning effort.

Children begin to learn reading by sounding out the letters. As long as we deal with the very simplest cases like 'cat' and 'dog', 'mom' and 'dad', etc., they do well. Then, as we progress to multi-syllable words, the process comes to a grinding halt. Words that sound alike have different spellings and meanings. Letters and letter combinations are pronounced differently in different words. Some letters are silent. Several different letters can sound the same depending on the word they are used in. All the time we spend learning spelling and pronunciation stands in the way of extracting the knowledge in the educational materials we are trying to learn how to read.

Here's a little demonstration of how the mind works. This is not a trick. Have several people try it. Count aloud the number of F's in the following sentence, and write down the total. Count them only once.

FINISHED FILES ARE THE RE
SULT OF YEARS OF SCIENTIF
IC STUDY COMBINED WITH
THE EXPERIENCE OF YEARS

Now read the footnote at the bottom of the page. [1]

---

[1] Most people will count three F's even though there are six. The F's in 'OF' are perceived as V's, which is how they sound. The mind, which is phonetic, must translate them.

The English language is grammatically simpler than many others, but it is more difficult to gain proficiency in it because it is so memory intensive. The following examples should make the point:

- Words with nearly identical spelling sound different: bomb, comb and tomb; bough, cough, rough;

- Words that sound the same are spelled differently: air and err; bear and bare; beer and bier; bury and berry; deer and dear; do, dew and due; doe and dough; done and dun; dual and duel; draft and draught; hew, hue, and whew; hoar and whore; meat, meet and mete; per and purr; root and route, or rout and route; to, too, and two, etc., etc.

- Double letters are used when they are not sounded separately: abbot, arrow, illicit, pinnacle.

- Words that sound exactly alike have different meanings: matter and madder; bear and bare. Bear can be an animal, or it can mean 'to carry' or 'to tolerate'. Bare can be an adjective or verb meaning either 'exposed' or 'to expose'.

- Letter combinations are used to make sounds for which we already have single letters: photo, phrase, physics, laugh, cough. We already have the letter 'f' which sounds just like the combinations 'ph' and 'gh', why do we need the combinations? The same is true for the letter combination 'ck': clock, kick, pluck, rock. Since the 'c' and 'k' ending these words sound alike, what is the purpose of having them both? Another example is character and charisma. When we have the letter 'k' available, why do we need to use the 'ch' as a 'k' sound?

- Some letter combinations can have two different pronunciations: character and charter; charity and charisma.

- Two different letters can be pronounced the same: size, wise; waiter, wader. Why should an 's' sound like a 'z', or a 't' like a 'd'?

- Two different letters often are pronounced the same: celestial, selection; cell, sell. Why do we need a 'c' to sound like an 's' that we already have available?

NO CHILD LEFT BEHIND

- Some letters cannot be individually sounded: quick, quake; extra and xylophone. Since the letter 'q' sounds like the combination 'kw', and the letter 'x' sounds like 'ks', 'kz' or 'gz', why do we need these letters? Would they not be better used for sounds not represented by our existing alphabet?

- These and very many other words contain letters which are not sounded: cologne, foam, pier, pique, etc. Why do we need silent letters? What purpose do they serve?

- In some words, two different letters have the same sound: mystic. Why should the 'y' and 'i' sound alike?

- In other words, the same letter has two or more different sounds: reenter, reexamine

- The various forms used to communicate plurality merely add confusion to the English language: cat, cats; cannon, cannon; octopus, octopi; mouse, mice; goose, geese; is, am, are. . A common standard would simplify matters and accelerate learning. Why should the verb need to be plural when the noun already conveys plurality?

- We have many ways of expressing groupings in the animal world: flock of sheep, gaggle of geese, herd of buffalo, pack of wolves, pride of lions, pod of whales, etc. Why do we need all these ways of expressing what is essentially a group, family, clan, tribe, or herd?

Look through the dictionary. You will find many cases like these. One should not have to memorize the spelling and pronunciation of every word in order to be able to read it. Nor should one be dependent upon seeing a complete sentence to determine the context and meanings of the words in it. This factor is a major obstacle to developing people (and computers) that understand human speech and writing.

I don't expect people will flock to the idea, but if English became a phonetic language, every child of normal intelligence would be able to read by the age of three or four. There would be no need to learn spelling and pronunciation would be obvious. Early reading would enable early learning. National programs to revise how a language is written are not without precedent. In 1928, Mustafa Kemal Ataturk, first president of Turkey, began the conversion of Turkey's alphabet from the Arabic to a modified Latin one similar to those used by many European countries. The task was completed in four years.

NO CHILD LEFT BEHIND

The result was a phonetic alphabet better able to express Turkish words. The change I am proposing is far simpler than the one he undertook, since it is merely a matter of establishing rules for pronunciation of individual letters and letter combinations. We have computers that can automatically translate everything ever written into the new form. That would spawn an entirely new industry.

It has been estimated that 92% of college graduates are working outside their field of study. There are a number of reasons that may be deduced from this. We view high school as preparation for college, and college as preparation for the working world. Most high school students have no idea of what career they are best suited for, which occupations are most in demand, which pay a decent wage, what their future financial needs will be, how to manage their finances, and which occupation they might actually enjoy. This is a major failing of our secondary education system. Part of the explanation may be that the failures of the primary education system force high schools to teach what should have been learned in elementary school. That, in turn, forces colleges to spend two years teaching what should have been learned in high school.

Earlier, we mentioned a cafeteria system to determine elementary school students' areas of interest and aptitude. A similar system is needed in high school to help students decide on a career. During the first two years, one class could be devoted to exploring career choices. In the last two years, during part of their four breaks from school, students could do one-week internships, with or without pay, in industries in which they have some interest. That would require schools to partner with businesses and institutions. The ability to experience varied work environments should make the career decision much easier for students. More people ultimately working in the field they studied would raise the competence of employees. That assumes that they have an opportunity to go on to college. About one-fourth of high school students fail to graduate, and one third of those that do graduate do not go on to college. That means that nearly half of our high school students will become part of a permanent underclass.

Have you wondered why we have a shortage of college graduates in engineering, sciences, mathematics, medicine, and other demanding disciplines? We have exported the technical jobs to other countries, and driven down wages here by bringing in lower-paid foreign technical

NO CHILD LEFT BEHIND

workers. The brain drain from those countries deprives them of their best and brightest, and deprives our best and brightest of good opportunities. The better schools are out of reach for most students. Too many college graduates have difficulty finding jobs in their own field, or jobs in their own field that pay enough to repay their student loans. Why undertake a difficult course of study if it does not improve your prospects? As an example, our nursing shortage is being addressed by importing lower-paid foreign nurses. Our nursing schools do not graduate enough nurses to meet demand. They cannot get enough qualified teachers because the pay is often less than they can earn as nurses.

Just as specialization based on student interest and ability and specialization in teaching would improve education, it might have a similar effect if universities were more highly specialized around disciplines. The cost of a university education might be considerably lower if they were organized around occupational domains like medical, law, physics, chemistry, information technology, engineering, music, etc. In some of these technical fields, the rate of change is so great that much of what is learned becomes obsolete before a degree is earned. Specialization would make it easier for universities to stay more current in their chosen fields. The rate of change, facilities and equipment requirements, and cost for subjects like political science, history, sociology, theology, communications, marketing, and others, could be much lower. With rare exceptions, the proliferation of for-profit, online or on-campus, unaccredited, and lower cost colleges does little to advance knowledge in technical fields or employability of their students.

We are at an important crossroad. Our future prosperity depends on high quality jobs. They, in turn, depend on innovation, and innovation depends on education. Consider the number of industries that have been spawned by technological innovations in the past century. Education enables research and development of new products and technologies that will provide high paying jobs of tomorrow. In the short term, we need to focus our energies on rebuilding our infrastructure. The jobs thus created will pay for our schooling while we wait for that education to bear fruit. Even with those interim jobs, the earnings will be inadequate to pay for a sufficient number of advanced degrees. How can we make up the difference? There is enough waste, fraud, and abuse in our system that we could easily provide an associate degree or trade school certificate to every student with the ability and

NO CHILD LEFT BEHIND

desire to pursue higher learning. Implementing the gross revenues tax system would enable us to do even more and pay down the national debt. Only one thing stands in our way: political ideology. We think it fitting that taxpayers provide an education to many military personnel, yet the very notion of doing it for our other best and brightest immediately raises red flags. Therein lies the dilemma: our choice is between political ideology and regaining our technological advantage in the world. You get to choose.

Education is the most powerful weapon which you can use to change the world.
Nelson Mandela

Democracy cannot succeed unless those who express their choice are prepared to choose wisely. The real safeguard of democracy, therefore, is education.
Franklin D. Roosevel

Sooner or later, we will have to recognise that the Earth has rights, too, to live without pollution. What mankind must know is that human beings cannot live without Mother Earth, but the planet can live without humans.

Evo Morales

RACE TO SPACE

Over the past decades, we have spent fortunes trying to get off this planet. To some it may seem like a horrible waste of our resources. Billions of dollars went into going to the moon, sending satellites to other planets, and building a space station in which people can live for short periods of time. What for? Any habitable planet is many light years from here. No technology exists that will enable us to reach it anytime within the next few centuries. Why would we want to get there? **We may not have a choice because The rate at which we are gobbling up our natural resources and destroying our environment makes it imperative.** The population of the world has tripled since I was born, and it will continue to grow although at a somewhat slower pace. More than 7 billion people now share space on this rock. All of them require air to breathe, water, food, shelter, and fuel for heat, cooking, and transportation.

We behave as if these resources are unlimited. No thought is given to what our children and their progeny will need to survive here. Only about three percent of the earth's surface is arable land (usable for growing food), much of which requires irrigation. Very few plants used for food can thrive in salt water, and fresh water resources are diminishing worldwide. Water can be desalinated, but the technology is much too costly to use for irrigation.

Much of the land beneath us was under a sea at some point in the very distant past. Modern horizontal drilling techniques for oil and gas, aimed at increasing output, force water and chemicals under very high pressure into the drilled channels to fracture oil and gas bearing rocks to release their valuable contents. It is called fracking. The water pumped in dissolves the salt deposits that have been buried for millions of years. Salinated water is released into rivers, creeks, and irrigation wells contaminating the soil and destroying the vegetation that feeds us and our livestock. Consequently, once productive farming areas in Montana and other states are no longer useful for most food crops.

Several television news reports showed flammable well water coming out of faucets in areas of Colorado where these techniques were being employed. A spark would cause the effluent to burn. Non-stop advertizing by the industry claims hydraulic fracturing is the safe answer to our nation's energy independence. But, at what cost? Our fresh water reserves are being contaminated. Texas, Oklahoma, and other areas that have been extensively fracked are experiencing frequent earthquakes due to tidal forces, the gravitational pull on the earth's crust by our sun and moon.

The air is also getting polluted. I have been in cities of China and Taiwan when the air was so polluted that it was unbreathable during rush hours, people had to wear masks, and throat cancers were common. Fracking releases methane and other pollutants into the atmosphere. Methane is a toxic substance that contributes to global warming and respiratory diseases. It is also the natural gas we use to cook our food and heat our homes. The Obama administration enacted clean air regulations that require the oil and gas industry to test for methane leaks and prevent the escape of methane from leaking. We have the technology to do so, but it would add some cost. The Trump administration is striking down various components of the clean air act.

A billion vehicles, airplanes, ships, power plants, and heat sources are powered by fossil fuels. All of them are spewing heat and tons of pollutants into the atmosphere, which are causing global warming and climate change. There is no doubt that global ice caps are melting causing ocean waters to rise. We have satellite photographs showing miles of ice caps disappearing at the poles over the last fifty to sixty years. Flooding has become a worldwide problem, as has the incidence of severe weather. These have always been with us, but never as widespread and severe in recorded history. Scientists at the National Oceanographic and Atmospheric Administration (NOAA) have tracked the amount of carbon dioxide (CO^2) released into the atmosphere for decades. A majority of scientists agree that the rise in CO^2 correlates closely with the increase in global temperatures. Yet, the oil, gas, and electrical power generating industries have somehow managed to stifle their voices, claiming that these are merely natural weather cycles. Even if that were true, should we not be trying to avert these global catastrophes? Once again, money and politics trump common sense.

Plants consume CO^2, use the carbon for their growth, and release the oxygen that we breathe. Forests are the most efficient purifiers. At the same time as our emission of greenhouse gasses increases, forests are being cut down to make room for agriculture. Japan alone has a sustainable forestry program. We should remember that the Sahara, largest desert on earth, was once a lush tropical paradise. I highly recommend Jared Diamond's book, *Collapse: How Societies Choose to Fail or Survive*, in which he discusses current and past examples of short-sightedness that led to collapse of various civilizations.

When my wife and I were traveling in Europe, we rented a Volvo with a smart diesel engine. We drove it through Germany at about 100 miles per hour for about 700 miles. It got 46 miles per gallon. The engine shut off every time we came to a stop and started running the instant the accelerator was pressed. I believe it also shut off cylinders that were not needed to maintain our selected speed. On another leg of the trip, we rented a Ford C-Max that gave us 36 miles per gallon, about double what my Ford Explorer gets here. That technology is available. The Obama administration passed new fuel mileage standards that would nearly double the mileage we currently get. The Trump administration overturned the regulation even though it would have given a significant boost to our auto industry and save American families a lot of money.

Every time gasoline tops $3.00 per gallon, politicians begin to speak of our addiction to oil. We are not addicted to oil; we just have not been given an alternative. I think it is more likely that our politicians are addicted to oil money. Otherwise our public transportation systems would not have been so neglected, and our vehicles would be fueled by something other than gasoline and diesel fuel. We need truly renewable energy sources. Unfortunately, research into alternative energy is controlled by the industry that is most threatened by it.

While we were in Brazil, all the cars were fueled with ethanol. A big deal has been made here of E85, or 85% ethanol and 15% gasoline. There is a lot about ethanol they do not tell you. To begin with, ethanol has approximately 60% of the energy content of gasoline. If your car gets 20 miles per gallon with gasoline containing the usual 12% ethanol, it will probably get about 14 mpg with E85' especially in larger and heavier vehicles. That means E85 should cost no more than $2.10 per gallon for you to break even. Ethanol is made from corn, the same corn that is used to feed livestock and dairy cows, and that provides about 40% of the calories we consume. The increased demand for corn due to ethanol production has already resulted in significant increases in food prices, in spite of the 51 cent per gallon subsidy to ethanol producers and farm subsidies to corn growers. There are far more cars here than in Brazil. There is no way to produce enough ethanol to meet our demand for motor fuel. Even if there was, a lot of fuel must be burned to produce ethanol, so the cost will always be unacceptably high. Research is underway to produce ethanol from wood. That would only speed up the destruction of our forests.

Diesel fuel is much like kerosene, heating oil, and jet fuel. It is much less refined than gasoline, and should be much cheaper to produce. Why then is it priced higher than gasoline? Diesel fuel also burns dirtier than gasoline, so its impact on the environment would be greater if more vehicles burned it. Bio-diesel, which has been promoted as fuel for vehicles, is vegetable oil, the stuff we use to deep-fry our foods. Some of it can come from discarded cooking oil, but no way is there enough of it to power a lot of vehicles. It does not provide a significant benefit to the environment because it is very similar to regular diesel fuel. Petroleum comes from rotted vegetation that has been buried in the earth for millions of years. Bio-diesel also comes from vegetation, but is captured before it is buried. If it were to be more widely used, food prices would increase even more.

The other problem with petroleum-based fuels is that petroleum is needed for other uses and it will ultimately be depleted. Most of our plastics are petroleum based, as are many of the chemicals we use. Allowing it to be depleted would drive up the cost of most products. Aluminum is abundant, but it takes a tremendous amount of energy to produce. Glass is very abundant and requires less energy to produce, but we need to research ways of modifying its properties to make it more suitable for most consumer goods. In the end, other materials would have to be discovered. Plastics can be made from the cellulose in trees and various plants, but that would increase the rate at which we destroy our forests. Plant based fuels pose another problem — soil depletion. Farmers know that crops must be rotated to preserve the soils capacity to provide adequate quality and quantity of food. So much of our food comes from corn and soy beans that it becomes extremely difficult, if not impossible, to rotate those crops. Dedicating more land to ethanol production will, in the long run, threaten our food supply.

Chemical fertilizers can boost yields, but have several downsides. The nitrogen in them is derived from natural gas, which is another resource that can be depleted. Nitrogen based fertilizers are mostly nitrogen, phosphorus, and potassium. Some may contain other so-called macronutrients and even a few micronutrients. No one really knows the effect of long-term use of chemical fertilizers. They drain into rivers and are carried into oceans. How they will affect marine life, which is already being depleted by overfishing, global warming, and pollution remains to be seen. Algae blooms are currently killing much marine life in the west of Florida. No one knows for sure what effect the Gulf of Mexico oil spill, Exxon Valdez incident, and dozens of other spills into our oceans and waterways will have on our food chain.

The holy grail of vehicular fuel is hydrogen. Hydrogen has higher energy content than gasoline, so fuel mileage would be significantly improved. Hydrogen fuel cells have been powering electrical systems on spacecraft for decades. They could just as easily power electric cars. Initially, hydrogen could power existing cars with internal combustion engines. There are two ways to get hydrogen. We can get it from natural gas in a process akin to what is used to extract nitrogen, or we can get it from water, the most abundant resource on earth. The beauty of hydrogen is that burning it produces only water. It is the most environmentally friendly fuel. It produces no carbon dioxide, so contributes very little to global warming. There are a few technical issues to be resolved, and the oil companies are pursuing solutions, but they are pursuing solutions they can control.

You don't need oil wells to get gasoline when you can get water from the ocean. There are two ways to approach the problem. One company is developing hydrogen generators to be placed in gas stations. You would simply refill your tank much like refilling a propane cylinder for your barbecue grill, or you could just exchange cylinders. The other way is to build a small hydrogen generator right into your vehicle. Of course, then you would not need a gas station. Imagine that, no gas stations, no oil companies involved, no $4.00/gallon gas. Condensers could be used to recapture much of the water. The result would be as yet unimaginable fuel mileage. Your car would cost a bit more, and would require periodic maintenance, but the total cost to you would be much less. Why do you think your car is not already powered by hydrogen?

Vehicular fuel consumption is only part of the problem. Equally serious is industrial, commercial, governmental, and home energy consumption. Coal fired power plants supply most of the electrical needs of our country. Coal is plentiful, but it is the dirtiest to burn, mining it is dangerous, and it generates tremendous amounts of greenhouse gases that contribute to global warming. They can be cleaned up considerably by installing scrubbers to remove some of the pollutants. The limits on CO^2 emissions from coal fired power plants enacted by the Obama administration have been struck down by the Trump administration in order to save the coal industry. It will not save that industry because gas is a much cheaper way to generate power. It flows out of the ground to the point of use. It does not need to be transported by train or handled many times in the process. All it will do is increase pollution.

Power plants fueled by oil or natural gas are subject to the same price manipulation as gasoline. Oil and coal fired plants are dirty. Natural gas burns cleaner, but both are depletable resources better used for other purposes. That leaves us with two alternatives: natural power sources and conservation. Natural power sources include hydroelectric, geothermal, wind, and solar. They might be adequate to meet our demands for electricity if we eliminate much of the waste. The earth has a hot core of molten iron. Gravitational force and friction from slippage of the continental plates assures that it will remain molten for a long time. Steam from that heat can be used to power turbine generators without need for any fuel, and with no pollution whatsoever. Geothermal power plants are much less costly than nuclear ones. All that is needed is a water source. All the electrical power needs of the island nation of Iceland are supplied by geothermal power plants. There are many locations in the United States with access to geothermal energy, including

Arkansas, Colorado, and Wyoming. Wind power is being used around the world for generating electricity and is gaining in the U.S. Aside from being a bit of an eyesore, and somewhat variable in output, they are environmentally friendly. The Netherlands and other countries are successfully using wind-powered generators to supply much of their needs. There is no reason for us not to do the same. Hydroelectric power is also a low cost way of generating electricity. It does not pollute the air, but it does have some environmental impact. Dams also prevent silt from traveling downstream. Silt is important for supporting marine life and building buffer zones in coastal areas to protect against storm surges. Dams can also prevent the migration of some fish species. My personal dream for energy independence is a combination of solar power and any other technology that would enable us to disconnect from utility companies. One option might be a hydrogen fuel cell capable of supplying all the power a home might need. It would eliminate much of the costly to build and maintain power grid that is so vulnerable to terrorist attack.

A few years ago, a tsunami in Japan killed thousands of people and caused three of four reactors at the Fukushima Daiichi nuclear power plant to melt down releasing radioactive matter into the air and water and causing the government to evacuate all residents within thirteen miles of the plant. The area remains in crisis for an undetermined amount of time. Nuclear power plants have been touted as being the cleanest, safest, and lowest cost source of electricity. You probably could not tell that to the folks at Fukushima, Chernobyl or Three Mile Island. Nuclear power plants cost billions to build. They do not normally produce air pollution. When nuclear fuel rods are spent, they remain radioactive. We have no absolutely safe way on earth to store them. They may remain radioactive for thousands of years. The desire of terrorist organizations to acquire nuclear materials speaks against their proliferation. Has anyone not noticed the dramatic increase in various cancers in recent years?

As nuclear plants age, accidents become more likely. Exposure to radioactivity can be deadly rather quickly. In the United States, nuclear power plants which were built to a useful life limit of 40 years, are being relicensed for an additional 20 years, often without proper safety reviews or much public attention. No applications for renewals have been rejected. Regulators and the industry contend that there is no technical limit on the useful life of nuclear power plants. Some in the industry are planning for additional license extensions to 80 or even 100 years. An Associated Press report states that "Records show that paperwork of the U.S. Nuclear Regulatory Commission sometimes matches word-for-word the language used in a plant operator's application for renewal."

In the two World Wars, we sank many German submarines. The batteries contained mercury, which is very toxic to humans. Now, we are routinely cautioned to avoid consuming more than small quantities of ocean fish because of their mercury content, even though fish in the diet reduce the risk of heart disease. When will we ever learn? We tell our kids not to play with fire, yet we do so all the time.

Many chemical compounds cause serious injury or death. One such chemical is the pesticide chlorpyrifos banned by the EPA under the Obama administration because it causes brain and neurological damage. The Trump administration is trying to allow continuing its use in commercial farming in spite of a federal judge's ruling that it must be banned. Apparently the judge was smart enough to understand the science presented to him.

The Air Force operates fire fighting aircraft out of Peterson Air Force base in Colorado Springs to drop fire suppressing chemicals on wildfires. Cleanup of inevitable spills washed the chemicals off the tarmac into surrounding soils. It found its way into the wells supplying water to the neighboring town of Fountain making the water undrinkable. It took nearly two years to make the water drinkable again. Another example involved a family who were members of our church. The husband was an Air Force officer at a Montana intercontinental ballistic missile base in Montana. A transformer cooled with PCBs exploded. Nearly everyone who was exposed to the chemical died of cancer, including the husband. The wife and two children, who were not directly exposed, suffered the same fate within about two years.

There is no effective way to dispose of many dangerous chemicals. There are also many for which we do not have safer alternatives. Material safety data sheets are available for many, but they only help us if the suppliers provide them with each shipment and we read them and use and dispose of them properly. If a substance is dangerous but not easily deactivated, we should mandate that the manufacturer provide a neutralizing agent to quickly render it inert. Instead of dismantling the Environmental Protection Agency (EPA), we should be demanding that it test all powerful chemicals, food products and additives, and materials for safety on rodents.

Not all chemicals kill instantly. Many cause birth defects, cancers, and other maladies that become apparent over time. They must be detected through statistical analysis of those exposed over time. Many of them are so powerful that they can cause damage at incredibly small amounts in the parts per billion and parts per trillion ranges. Asbestos, which was used for many decades as pipe insulation, in brake and clutch linings, and myriad other uses, was banned because many of those working in proximity to it were dying of a particular form of cancer, mesothelioma. We painted our buildings with paints containing lead for more than a century before we realized it was toxic. Some of my friends who fought in the Vietnam war were disabled by exposure to the defoliant "agent orange" sprayed by bombers to kill the jungle vegetation in which enemy troops were concealed. The cleanup following the 9/11 terrorist attack in New York left many first responders permanently disabled or dead. Was it not the pollution in the air that sickened them?

It is high time for our government to take back the lead in energy research. I believe that hydrogen is our best shot at energy independence in the short term. In the longer term, finding the keys to understanding and controlling gravity is our best hope for reducing fuel cost, saving our environment, and making long space voyages practical. Perhaps the secret will be found in the dark energy that pushes galaxies apart in an expanding universe. The oil/gas/coal/energy companies have no interest in lowering our costs or saving our environment. They are cost-plus businesses concerned only with their own profits. If we truly want energy independence, the solution lies not only with independence from foreign countries but independence from oil/gas/coal/energy companies. They will not easily relinquish their favored positions. As long as the political process is so dependent on money, the lobbyists will use our money to get favored treatment for their clients. We can only achieve energy independence by taking back our government.

That is exactly what we must do to protect our health and safety as well. We cannot accomplish that unless we find an alternative to the two failed ideologies that brought us to this point. Life expectancy has begun to decline in the US for the first time in decades, substance abuse is at epidemic levels, we imprison more people than any nation on earth, violence is rampant, homeless and poor are everywhere, and the people that promised to make America great again forgot to include about ninety percent of us. We have far more to fear from disease, violence, natural disasters, poverty, and the monsters that we create than we do from terrorists.

Congress, you must decide the future course of the United States that I passionately love. It rescued me from the Soviets and the Nazis, and I owe it my life. It is now in need of rescue.

Federal elections happen every two years in this country. Presidential elections every four years. And four years just isn't long enough to dismantle all the environmental laws we've got in this country.
Jared Diamond

FREEDOM OF RELIGION

We continually play with our language to make our words more pleasing or innocuous. "Lady' once meant woman of noble birth or refined manners; now, it is applied to any woman. A television news reporter recently referred to a murderer as 'that gentleman'. 'Personnel Department' is now 'Human Resources'. 'Used' is now 'pre-owned'. 'Gay' once meant carefree and joyful. Now it means 'homosexual'. 'Right to work' now may mean 'right for employers to fire indiscriminately'. 'Politics' was once related to 'polite' or 'civilized'; now, it is anything but. The same is true with 'freedom of religion'. It originally meant we should be free to practice whatever religion we choose. The state could not dictate the religion we were to believe or practice, and no religious institution could dictate government policy or laws. Its intent was to maintain a separation of church and state.

From earliest times, governments have tried to dictate what its subjects should believe. When Socrates taught that there was one God, The Greeks tried him for atheism, and sentenced him to drink poison. Religion and the state were intertwined. Heresy was akin to treason. The Romans were tolerant of other religions up to a point. Once per year, everyone was required to offer sacrifices to the Roman gods and the Emperor. Jews and Christians refused to do so. For a while Jews were exempted. Christians were brutally persecuted for nearly three centuries. Until the last three centuries, forcible conversion was a common practice. The Muslim religion was spread mostly by the sword. The Inquisitions were as much a political tool as religious oppression. Zwingli, leader of the Reformed Churches died in a war to forcibly convert Catholics. Martin Luther approved the burning of Anabaptists as blasphemers, the deportation of Jews to Palestine, or the burning of their synagogues. Calvinists killed Anabaptists in Switzerland. Catholics and Protestants were alternately persecuted and killed in England. Witch trials were a blot on the American continent and Europe. We should not judge past actions by today's standards.

In the eighteenth century, absolute monarchies began to be replaced by more democratic forms of government. Revolutions in the United States and France aimed to give individual citizens a voice. But, it was not quite that easy to separate church from state. The churches' role in preserving public morality was

FREEDOM OF RELIGION

replaced by civil and criminal laws. Prohibitions were imposed on drinking, drugs, prostitution, gambling, polygamy, homosexual activity, and indecency. They had little or no effect. Sects or cults proliferated under the banner of 'freedom of religion'. Instead of governments and churches imposing their religious will on the populace, people could impose their religious or irreligious will on governments and churches—forbidding prayer in schools, religious observance in public places, etc.

A man in California sued to have the phrase 'one nation under God' removed from the Pledge of Allegiance. He tried to use the Constitution to accomplish what the Constitution forbids — forcing his belief on everyone else. No one compels him or his child to utter that phrase. Why should he be able to compel others not to? They could simply say 'under me' if they chose to. If there is no harm, there is no foul. If one does not believe in a supreme being, is he not his own god?

In another case, a judge resigned his position rather than remove a statue bearing the Ten Commandments from a courthouse. No one was compelled to read the Ten Commandments. No one was compelled to believe that God exists, or anything else for that matter. No symbol of any particular religion was displayed. The government was not forcing us to believe anything. It was not setting up a state religion. The problem is that the proliferation of denominations, sects, and cults makes it extremely difficult to maintain fairness to all of them. In a pluralistic society, there could be dozens or even hundreds of groups wanting their symbols to be displayed, or services to be performed on public property. There is no practical way to accommodate them, so it is probably best to disallow all of them on public property. However, people should be free to display whatever religious symbols they wish on their own property. Whatever one calls a tree with decorations on it, it is a tree with decorations, not an official symbol of a religion. Our nation's capitol contains works of art depicting religious observance by various historical figures. Such historical representations of important figures in our history, even if they contain some religious symbols, are not the same thing as promoting their religion.

When the Russians, under Stalin, invaded eastern Poland in 1939, they imposed their atheistic belief on the populace. Churches were converted into warehouses and stables. Teaching of religion was prohibited. My mother was imprisoned briefly for defying their orders.

FREEDOM OF RELIGION

The Nazis who invaded Poland killed more than 9,000 Polish Catholic priests, six million Jews, and many millions of Poles and Russians. Both Hitler and Stalin attempted to replace religion with irreligion. Are not the people behind the Pledge of Allegiance case and similar efforts actually trying to do the same thing?

The reverse is also true. We want government to impose our doctrinal and moral standards on everyone, even when we ourselves fail to live up to them. For example, we want government to define what constitutes marriage, beginning of life, limits of decency, how we should teach the origins of man, and countless other issues. Government is made up of people like us. They don't know. All they can do is set minimum standards. It is up to churches and schools to set the bar higher, but, because they too are made up of people like us, they have had limited impact on our behavior. This is particularly true in the public school system where discipline and teaching of moral behavior has been abandoned.

I am a pro-life practicing Catholic and author of two books on the Bible. My religion is very important to me, but I am dismayed that it has been highjacked by politicians as a political tool.

The Pharisees and Sadducees of Jesus' day were the religious and civil authorities. One must wonder how the Sadducees came to control the religious establishment and temple worship when they had no belief in the afterlife or final judgment. Both considered themselves the ultimate authority. All reward and punishment happened in this life. Their upper class status was proof of God's favor. Poverty, illness, and misfortune were God's punishment for sin therefore they did not have to help the sinners. It was these upright pillars of society that demanded that Jesus be crucified. To them, the laws of Moses were absolute.

A group of scribes and Pharisees approached Jesus as he was teaching near the temple, bringing a woman they intended to stone to death after she was caught in adultery (John 8:1-11). They wanted to trap Jesus into defending her when their law clearly stated she and her partner in the act should be put to death (Lev 20:10). They had not brought the male offender. When they asked him what they should do, Jesus began writing in the dirt with his finger. They must have seen what Jesus was writing. A likely speculation is that Jesus was writing the names of their partners in adultery. He simply asked them to have the one without sin cast the first stone. When none of the accusers came forward, Jesus admonished the woman to go and sin no more. Jesus repeatedly stated that his objective was not punishment but to lead sinners to repentance and a virtuous life (Mt 9:13, Mk 2:17, Lk 5:32, 15:7).

Jesus was not a revolutionary in the traditional sense as some scholars have suggested. He was not trying to overthrow either Jewish or Roman civil authorities, who were obviously corrupt, but to wrest spiritual and religious authority from their grasp. The Jerusalem temple and its religious establishment had become a massive economic enterprise with its own currency, marketplace, and political appointees as high priests. It was not about saving souls or spreading the faith. Three of the Gospels tell of Jesus driving out the sacrificial animals, those selling them, and the money changers from the temple (Mt 21:12-13, Mk 11:15-17, Jn 2:13-16). This is likely the event that aroused the ire of Jewish religious authorities who were benefiting from the commercial activities.

There is a parallel between the situation of the woman caught in adultery and our discussion on abortion and contraception. Adultery was illegal just as abortion was before Roe vs Wade. The woman and her partner nevertheless committed adultery. And so did more than one million U.S. women annually have abortions while it was illegal. An average of 440,000 women each year had illegal abortions in this country, and about 600,000 travelled to other countries to have them where it was legal. All the law against adultery did was allowed the authorities to punish those who broke it. The law did nothing to change their behavior. It may have deterred a few people through fear, but little else.

All the rhetoric about overturning Roe vs Wade is just political theater to persuade us to vote a particular way. It has more to do with politics than with stopping abortion, first because it won't and second because the right to life is about much more than abortion. If we have a right to life, then we have a right to health care, retirement security, a living wage, protection from violence and disasters, and the death penalty should be abolished.

That one political party favors unrestrained abortion on demand, including late term partial birth abortions, is appalling. But, I also don't believe that we should force a woman who has been violently raped to pass on the rapists genes unless she chooses to have the child. Modern technology makes it possible to determine if a fetus is not viable, in which case an abortion should be permitted. With the ready availability of effective contraceptives, there is no excuse for unwanted pregnancies. Abortion is not an acceptable birth control technique.

The other party's attack on contraception as a religious freedom issue, driven by insurance companies wanting to avoid paying for them, is ludicrous when we consider that making contraceptives readily available to young people has significantly reduced the number of abortions. There is not one word from Jesus or anyone else in the Bible about contraception.

We believe the Church is correct in prohibiting sex before marriage. It allows us to give ourselves completely to our spouse. While its purpose is procreation, the pleasure of it adds much joy to marriage. God said: *"Be fertile and multiply; fill the earth and subdue it"* (Gen 1:28). Thank you, God, we have done that. Can we slow down now before we have exhausted everything you have given us? When he gave that command, there were few people on earth. I am sure God intended for us to manage it sustainably in perpetuity.

Over the centuries, girls were often married between the ages of fourteen and seventeen. It was reasonable to expect them to retain their virginity until married. Now more than half are unmarried living together and having babies. If and when they do marry, half of them divorce. By the time they leave high school, about 60% of teenagers have engaged in sexual activity, as have 15% before reaching high school, and 25% had some form of sexually transmitted disease, with human papilloma virus (HPV) that causes cervical cancer being most prevalent according to the Centers for Disease Control. The vast majority did not use any contraceptive devices. These young people are children of all faiths including ours.

If abstinence was easy, we would not have sexual abuse by Catholic priests and Protestant ministers (yes, them too). Jesus said that celibacy was a grace not given to all (Matt 19:11-12). While marriage does not guarantee freedom from sexual abuse, at least they would not have an excuse for their behavior if they had an outlet for their primal drive..

Economics plays a role in all this. Women are marrying in their late twenties and having their first child in their early thirties. The cost of apartments, weddings, and college debt is largely responsible for the delay. About a third of young people continue to live with their parents into their thirties. Many others are sharing group apartments or homes. You can see that it is government policies that have contributed to the erosion of the nuclear family.

FREEDOM OF RELIGION

Several of my college educated fundamentalist evangelical friends insist the earth is 6,000 years old, that God created man instantaneously in finished form, and that Adam and Eve were the first humans, and that many early characters in the Bible lived for hundreds of years. I point out to them that the earliest Sumerian king lists recorded the length of reign of eight kings who ruled between 3500 BC and 2900 BC as 241,000 years. Clearly, the reigns were recorded in days using the Sumerian base sixty system of mathematics. The word for year simply changed meaning. The book of Genesis was most likely written down close to that period. Furthermore forensic scientists have examined many tens of thousands of ancient remains. None appear to have lived beyond our life expectancy. They live in a world of alternative facts and invent convoluted explanations to support their beliefs.

In their eyes, God is somehow diminished if he used natural evolutionary processes to create man. In 1917, the state of Tennessee actually convicted John T. Scopes, a high school coach and substitute teacher, of teaching evolution and fined him about $1,500 in today's dollars. Apparently, they had not understood what they read in the book of Genesis.

Gen 1:24. *Then God said,* **"Let the earth bring forth all kinds of living creatures:**

Gen 2:4-7. *Such is the story of the heavens and the earth at their creation. At the time when the LORD God made the earth and the heavens--* **while as yet there was no field shrub on earth and no grass of the field had sprouted**, *for the LORD God had sent no rain upon the earth and there was no man to till the soil, but a stream was welling up out of the earth and was watering all the surface of the ground,* **the LORD God formed man out of the clay of the ground and blew into his nostrils the breath of life**, *and so man became a living being.*

Science says that man originated as a one-celled creature in the primordial mud precisely as the Bible states. It was not in final form that God created man. If God had formed man in final form before plants and animals, man would have starved. It is clear in Genesis 1:28-30 that God gave dominion to man over all plants and animals, which God had created first. **God created man through evolution**. Several passages say that **everything changes (evolves), but God does not change.** God, the author of science, works through it.

Adam and Eve's first children were two sons. Cain was a farmer and Abel was a shepherd. We have archaeological evidence that organized farming began after the last ice age at about 9,000 BC. Sheep and Goats were first domesticated soon after. We have found human remains that predate them by thousands of years. Adam and Eve were not the first humans. After Cain killed his brother Abel, he was banished from his family. The Bible tells us that he married, had several children, and founded a city. If Adam, Eve, and Cain were the only people on earth, where would Cain have found a wife? We can choose to believe in fables or we can understand that the story of Adam and Eve represents man evolving from a naked hunter gatherer to one wearing leather garments, beginning farming and raising livestock, and becoming aware of God. We quit believing the world was flat when overwhelmed by evidence to the contrary. It's time to base all our beliefs based on evidence and common sense.

The book of Revelation contains many prophecies of environmental disasters. There is significant evidence that they have begun and a vast majority of scientists agree that crisis is looming. For example, the Bible warns of the pollution of our waterways and oceans, destruction of marine life, and pollution of fresh water sources:

> **Rev 16:4**. *The third angel poured out his bowl on the rivers and springs of water. These also turned to blood.*
>
> **Rev 16:3**. *The second angel poured out his bowl on the sea.* ***The sea turned to blood like that from a corpse; every creature living in the sea died.***

The angels in these visions of John the Evangelist are incidental to these prophecies. A fundamentalist might focus on the angels, but it is we who are the angels of destruction to our environment. Those reading these prophecies in John's day did not have the scientific knowledge to understand biological warfare or manmade pollution, otherwise they would not have connected their sewers to their rivers.

Pursuing our short term interests may very well bring on the famines predicted in the Bible.

> **Rev 6:56**. *I heard what seemed to be a voice in the midst of the four living creatures. It said,* "***A ration of wheat costs a day's pay, and three rations of barley cost a day's pay****. But do not damage the olive oil or the wine."*

FREEDOM OF RELIGION

Jer 24:10. *I will send upon them the sword, famine, and pestilence, until they have disappeared from the land which I gave them and their fathers.*

If they will not listen to the scientists, perhaps they should listen to the Bible's end time prophecies concerning global warming:

Isaiah 30:26. *The light of the moon will be like that of the sun and the light of the sun will be seven times greater* (like the light of seven days). On the day the LORD binds up the wounds of his people, he will heal the bruises left by his blows.

Rev 16:8-9. *The fourth angel poured out his bowl on* **the sun. It was given the power to burn people with fire. People were burned by the scorching heat** *und blasphemed the name of God who had power over these plagues, but they did not repent or give him glory.*

It is baffling that a vast majority of Evangelical Christians are supporting an administration that is dismantling regulations put in place to protect all of us, reducing access to health care, enacting arbitrary and damaging trade policies, breaking international treaties, sowing divisions between people and nations, promoting fiscal irresponsibility, and undermining our faith in government. How does that comport with Jesus' final prayer for us:

> **John 17:11**. *And now I will no longer be in the world, but they are in the world, while I am coming to you.* ***Holy Father, keep them in your name*** *that you have given me, so* ***that they may be one just as we are***.

As **Christians** or people of any faith, we must all work for unity of persons, nations, ideologies, cultures, and religions. We must work for the good of all. That must be the purpose of all religions and reasonable people of no religion.

"I am tolerant of all creeds. Yet if any sect suffered itself to be used for political objects I would meet it by political opposition. In my view church and state should be separate, not only in form, but fact. Religion and politics should not be mingled."

Millard Fillmore (1809-1865) *13th U.S. President*

THE SECOND AMENDMENT

"<u>**A well regulated militia**</u> **being necessary to the security of a free state, the right of the people to keep and bear arms shall not be infringed.**"

I begin this chapter with the wording of the second amendment to the constitution because I am sure most gun owners have never actually read all the words or understood them. Most focus on the second half of that sentence without contemplating the first half, a well regulated militia.

James Madison in *Federalist Papers 46* explained that its purpose was to enable states to resist the military forces of an oppressive federal government. We have a right and perhaps a duty to form a well regulated militia when it becomes necessary. It also gives us the right to defend ourselves from attack by other persons.

Our states have National Guard units under the direction of their governors. We have seen them used in natural disasters and to support police in riots. They have also been used as reinforcements to our federal troops in our wars in Iraq and Afghanistan. They are our well-regulated militias.

It does not allow the formation of private militias that are not well regulated under the control of the state government. It does not grant any individual the right to own weapons of mass destruction (bombs, mortars, missiles, explosives, tanks, machine guns, etc.)

The National Rifle Association (NRA) was formed to protect our right to self defense, hunt game, and engage in shooting sports, all my reasons for owning and using firearms. I was a member of the NRA for more than forty-five years, a certified hunter education instructor, and occasionally competitive shooter. Over the years, the NRA became a political lobby whose emphasis became more on protecting firearms manufacturers than gun owners. I began to sour on the NRA when they fought to block the BATFE from imposing a limit on the number of weapons an individual could purchase at one time. Straw purchasers were buying fifty to one hundred weapons at a time and reselling them to drug cartels. Fighting against universal background checks and other common sense regulations after several mass shooting incidents was the last straw for me. I did not renew my membership. Nevertheless, I am a firm supporter of the second amendment.

In 1972, I went to work for a manufacturing company located four blocks from Cabrini Green, a notoriously dangerous housing project in Chicago. It is now long gone. People were being shot almost daily from the rooftops. I was hired to turn the business around, and that's what I was going to do. Two gangs, one Latino and one Black, were terrorizing the workforce. The previous manager lasted a few months and quit, a broken man. I couldn't quit. My wife and I had three children, one of whom was born with congenital defects and required frequent hospitalizations and medical attention. He was uninsurable, so we bore the cost out of pocket for six years, and were hopelessly in debt as a result. As an employee, I could get health insurance coverage for my family, the primary reason for leaving the management consulting business.

One of the worst offenders was a leader of one of the gangs. I caught him in the act of trying to knife my Production Manager. After I terminated him, another employee warned me that the manager and I were put on the gang's hit list. We were both to be killed. I thought they were idle threats, but over the next several days one employee was shot at behind the building, another was beaten and dumped in the front entrance, a carload of thugs tried to force me off the freeway, and then several hoodlums, apparently armed with rifles, were waiting on a railroad bridge above the freeway. I managed to evade both.

The police could not provide protection. I explained my concern for my family's well being. They suggested I vary my route home every day, check my car carefully, and avoid walking past doorways, around blind corners, and into alleys. If anyone suspicious approached, I was to run in the direction of the largest group of people and, if followed, I was to stay there and call the police. I frequently left after dark, our parking lot was in the alley, and the industrial area was deserted after normal work hours.

The uniformed police officers turned the case over to the gang crimes unit for further investigation. A few days later, I met with the gang crimes detectives. They confirmed that the threat was serious. The young man I had fired had a rap sheet that included twenty-seven juvenile arrests for violent crime. At the time of his termination, he was being tried for his first adult arrest, a broad daylight shotgun shoot-out with the police. Being a member of the inner council of his gang meant that he was a confirmed killer. The job was merely intended to display his best behavior during the trial.

I asked the officers "What can I do?" "Leave town", I was told. I explained why I couldn't do that, and asked for alternatives. "Do you want

THE SECOND AMMENDMENT

the official or the unofficial version?" The official version turned out to be the 'routes, alleys, doorways, corners, and crowds' speech. "What are the chances such measures will be enough?" "Not good", they replied. "If they want to get you, sooner or later they will."

The unofficial version went like this: "Buy a good gun, learn how to use it well, keep it with you at all times, and do all the other things we told you. Even then there are no guarantees." When I asked about applying for a permit to carry one, they replied "Don't waste your time. They're not issuing non-professional permits." I then asked, "Are you saying my only choice is to be a criminal or a victim?" They replied, "We don't make the laws. We just enforce them."

For days I struggled with their advice. Then, as I was driving with my wife and children in the car, returning from a visit with my parents, a terrible bang sent our hearts into our throats. There was no sensation of collision or a tire blowout. As I looked around, I saw a man clambering up an embankment holding a shiny pistol. We sped away. Upon arriving home, I inspected the car. On the right front vent window, there was a smear of lead where a bullet had ricocheted off the glass, and dug a groove in the door. We had been shot at. Had the shot come from a less acute angle, it would certainly have struck my wife in the chest. I shuddered at the thought of some mindless punk taking my wife's life, and robbing our children of their mother. I learned that day that protecting my family is my responsibility. The police cannot guard everyone who feels threatened, and they cannot be everywhere. A period of intensive self defense training followed.

I became my Production Managers bodyguard, taking him to work, to lunch, and back home for the next several months. The stress of those days had a severe impact on him. He developed serious heart disease, had a pacemaker installed, left my employ, went through a divorce, and was never quite the same. He died soon after. Our adversary was ultimately found guilty in the shootout trial, and was sent to prison. After several additional incidents, things quieted down.

The government not only failed to protect us, it tried to prevent us from protecting ourselves. The laws did nothing to prevent the criminals from being armed. Criminals, by their very nature, have a disregard for the law. Please don't tell me I must be a voluntary victim, or that I may not have the means to protect my family. That protection is my right and my obligation. Laws that deprive the decent citizen of means of protection do nothing to reduce violent crime. In fact, wherever citizens have been allowed to carry concealed firearms, violent crime has decreased. Most weapons of the past required a degree of physical prowess. Guns, on the other hand, can even be used by the aged and infirm. They are an equalizer.

There is craziness on both sides of the gun control debate. An **AR style rifle is not an assault rifle because it is not capable of fully automatic fire.** A civilian AR is just a semiautomatic rifle. When Illinois banned assault rifles in the 1990s, my most accurate semiautomatic version of the Israeli Galil military rifle would have cost me a mandatory year in prison if I had been caught with it. It was legal in Wisconsin and Michigan where I hunted. The people who wrote the law didn't know the difference between an assault rifle and a semiautomatic rifle.

In 2011, a young man wielding a 9mm pistol shot Congresswoman Gabrielle Giffords of Arizona in the head and wounded thirteen others including a nine year old girl. The pistol contained a 31 round magazine. What practical use is there for such a magazine other than for mass shootings? Several states passed laws restricting magazine capacity to fifteen rounds over the objections of the NRA. A reloading break might allow some brave soul to tackle a shooter, but it will not prevent the shooting.

My hearing has been permanently damaged by years of shooting. Silencers are now available for sale to civilians. In the past, their use has primarily been in clandestine assassinations. Why do civilians need them? They make a weapon not concealable, heavy, and unwieldy.

Last week, we stopped for dinner at a local restaurant. An elderly man in a cowboy hat was openly carrying a pistol on his hip. I call him and others like him muggee wannabe, those who invite a mugging. They obviously have not read about the many cops that get shot with their own pistols. In the self defense course I conduct for friends, I suggest that a weapon never be revealed unless there is imminent danger. It is never used to frighten, threaten, or impress anyone.

One response to recent school shootings has been to arm teachers. Not everyone, including teachers, has the mindset that would allow them to pull the trigger on another person, even one shooting at people. That requires training. Most concealed carry courses don't really provide it. You never get to handle a pistol or shoot it. Some of my friends with concealed carry permits have only test fired their pistols once and have never disassembled or cleaned them.

I believe that all citizens including teachers who want to have a concealed carry permit should be allowed to have one once they have had a comprehensive course with the weapon of their choice. It should cover safety and legal issues, methods of comfortable concealment, clearing malfunctions, ammunition types, stance, aiming, draw and fire drills on silhouette targets, disassembly, cleaning, and safe storage. They should then be required to qualify by hitting a six inch target zone on a target several times at a distance of thirty feet before receiving their permit. They should also be required to requalify prior to renewing their permits.

Most states require hunters to complete a hunter safety education course before obtaining their first hunting license. It has significantly reduced the number of accidental shootings and firearm accidents. I recommend that a similar course be required before the purchase of one's first firearm. You are prohibited from driving a car without a driver's license out of concern for public safety. Should we not also treat firearms with the same concern?

In the chapter on No *Child Left Behind,* we covered the importance of structure in raising children. A child who never hears "no", "we can't afford it", or "that is unacceptable behavior" rarely develops coping skills that enable it to deal with others' authority or not getting their own way. Parents' failure to exercise parental authority or provide moral or religious instruction may be largely responsible for many of the school shootings in recent years, many of which occur in middle class or upscale communities.

All that having been said, there will always be a few suffering from substance abuse or mental illness that are prone to violence. That is why comprehensive mental health care has to become part of our health care system. A mechanism must be put in placc to communicate potentially violent persons' identities to the authorities so they show up on mandatory background checks when they attempt to buy firearms.

"Laws that forbid the carrying of arms ... disarm only those who are neither inclined nor determined to commit crimes ... Such laws make things worse for the assaulted and better for the assailants; they serve rather to encourage than to prevent homicides, for an unarmed man may be attacked with greater confidence than an armed man."

Thomas Jefferson quoting from *On Crimes and Punishment* by criminologist Cesare Beccaria, 1764.

CRIMINAL JUSTICE

Ask anyone what the purpose of prisons is, and you will likely get one of two responses: to punish criminals (repaying a debt to society) or to rehabilitate them. Neither premise works. about half of those released from jail wind up back in jail or prison within three years. Apparently, they have not been rehabilitated, nor punished severely enough to be deterred from further criminal activity. That should lead one to conclude that some of the principles underlying our penal system may be wrong.

Through most of recorded history, systems of justice revolved around punishment. It was intended as a deterrent, but I suspect that desire for revenge played a part. It did nothing to help the victims of crime, and merely angered the perpetrator against society. To counter this anger, reformers introduced the concept of rehabilitation, the premise that treating criminals well will somehow motivate them to abandon their evil ways. Providing exercise yards, workshops, televisions, conjugal visits, and other amenities has done absolutely nothing to stem the criminal tide. The freedoms accorded prisoners have turned prisons into universities for crime, and increased the cost of operating them.

A television report a few years ago on Richard Speck, now-deceased mass murderer of eight student nurses, showed a video made by Speck and two other inmates. In the video, Speck was interviewed by his homosexual lover, described the murders in some detail, denied any remorse, snorted cocaine from an ample supply, was said to have engaged in sex acts on video (although that portion was edited out), and displayed a large hoard of cash which, presumably, he had earned by selling liquor he had brewed in jail. How is it possible that all these activities can take place in jail? The guards and prison administrations must either be intimidated, involved, or oblivious to what is happening on their watch. The prisons appear to be run by gangs, the same gangs that wreak havoc on our streets. Their influence extends beyond the prison walls. The inmate who might have a tendency to go straight cannot avoid being dragged into drugs, sex, theft, and violence.

Prisons are being privatized in an attempt to reduce costs. There are now more than 260 private prisons in the US, most of which are operated by three companies, and most of them are located in the South and West. It is noteworthy that the incarceration rate in several southern states is much higher than elsewhere in the country. There is no way of knowing whether the concentration of private prisons is somehow responsible for the high incarceration rate. Race alone does not appear to be a driving factor. About the only generalization that can be made is that incomes are generally lowest in southern states and highest in the northeast.

The annual cost per inmate is often higher in private prisons than in state run prisons, even though private prisons avoid getting the sickest and costliest inmates. That leads me to question the motivation of the judges filling these private prisons. Outsourcing the management of prisons to for-profit companies, which may hire low-wage guards with little or no training or background checks, is a very bad idea. It guarantees continued gang dominance, abuse of prisoners by other prisoners and guards, frequent escapes, and riots. Such prisons do not provide an environment capable of rehabilitating prisoners. If we really want to reduce cost, we should release the drug addicts and put them into mandatory drug rehabilitation programs. Even that will not help if we do not find better ways to reintegrate them into society.

Capital punishment has been with us since the beginning of recorded history, but there is not one shred of evidence to suggest that it deters crime. A vast majority of criminologists agree that executions do not lower the homicide rate. The state of Texas executes more criminals than any other state, but the murder rate is higher than in states that do not allow the death penalty. It also has one of the highest incarceration rates.

It has been estimated that it costs more to execute a criminal, including the cost of mandatory appeals, than to imprison for life. Only lawyers benefit from capital punishment. If it is not an effective deterrent to crime, and it is costlier than life in prison, we must question its effectiveness and morality, especially since DNA testing has demonstrated that many convicts are indeed innocent of the crimes for which they are imprisoned.

All too often we hear that a murderer has been imprisoned, served two to four years, was released, and then committed murder again. Parole hearings, presumably for determining if convicts have been sufficiently rehabilitated to be released, go on interminably. Victims and their relatives are forced to relive the horrors of the crimes repeatedly. Why? Remember the old radio program introduction, "Who knows what evil lurks in the minds of men? Only the Shadow knows!" Well, the Shadow is a fictional character. He does not sit on parole boards. I believe they should be eliminated. Ideally, mandatory fixed sentences should be imposed for each type of crime. Judges are subject to intimidation and corruption, like anyone else, and should be relieved of that burden. Repeat offenders should automatically receive a sentence double the previous one for each subsequent offense of the same kind. Generally, sentences for first time offenders could be much shorter.

Ex-convicts with a sincere desire to go straight upon release find themselves facing nearly insurmountable obstacles. Employers are reluctant to hire them. Those who come from dysfunctional or economically deprived families will find little help. Many suffer from diminished mental capacity, as well as emotional and psychological problems. Prospective employers and families alike shy away from them. One can find them among clients of homeless shelters. Even when they come from relatively normal backgrounds and are healthy, reintegration into society is extremely difficult. Complicate that with a substance abuse habit, and return to crime becomes the overwhelming probability. A program of education and career training during incarceration, mental health care, a guaranteed job and housing, and denial of access to harmful drugs would dramatically reduce the likelihood of reoffending.

Systems tend to change slowly even when based on faulty assumptions. Those in control have a vested interest in keeping things as they are. It is much easier to make relatively minor adjustments than to effect fundamental changes. The first change that must be made is in our attitude. Our motives must go from punishment or rehabilitation to the **protection of society.** Rehabilitation is a wonderful objective, but the only person that can bring it about or know that it has happened is the convict. We need to develop a new kind of prison that increases the probability of rehabilitation, costs less to operate, and prevents inmates and guards from abusing or corrupting each other.

The way to protect society from criminals is to isolate them from society — every kind of society: family, friends, public, professional, and criminal society. Inmates should have private cells that they never leave. The cells should give no opportunity for visual, voice, or personal contact with other inmates or guards. A simplified built-in computer terminal would provide for family and friends to visit from remote locations, a means of communicating with prison administrations regarding any special needs, and as an educational terminal. It should allow access to the news once or twice a day, and perhaps exercise programs, but not television programs or music that contain violent or otherwise objectionable material. Restricting the amount of time spent with sources of entertainment would almost certainly move the inmate to take advantage of educational programs, if only to avoid boredom. Making the programs such as correspondence courses interactive would permit testing and awarding of credits toward a college degree.

All the inmate's needs, including food, laundry, toiletries, should be supplied and removed through a blind opening in the wall, preferably by an automated system. Every effort should be made to provide a safe and pleasant environment, possibly including a small desk with writing materials, some exercise equipment, a chair, water cooler, toilet and shower. Nothing should be allowed into the cell from anyone outside the prison. That should prevent any kind of contraband from reaching any prisoner. All deliveries should be to cell numbers, not to prisoners by name. Maintaining the prisoner's anonymity is a way to insure the prisoner's safety and everyone's security.

There may be times when it is necessary to enter the prisoner's cell to perform repairs, provide medical care, or some other valid reason.

A dispatcher at a remote location should control all such access. Ideally, each cell should have a vestibule with an inner and outer door, only one of which can be open at one time. Closed circuit TV cameras in the cell, vestibule, and corridor should permanently document all access, but only while guards and service providers are accessing the cell or are inside. Their identities must be verified electronically at time of entry, in addition to being recorded on video and audio. Having access controllers selected at random at the beginning of each shift and maintaining prisoner anonymity should minimize the possibility of collusion to bypass security protocols. As you have probably figured out by now, such a prison could be operated with a much smaller staff, and would probably not require large walled compounds, workshops, guard towers, etc.

An inmate's stay would begin with indoctrination on how to use the equipment, what the educational choices are, what the rules and regulations are, what the consequences are for violating them, and the process for getting reintegrated into society. Near the end of the sentence, inmates would be required to return their cells to the condition in which they received them. Then, they would be allowed to work for a few weeks to service other inmates' needs in the kitchen, laundry, warehouse, or in janitorial services. Their performance and behavior during that period would determine whether they get released or returned to confinement. When released, they would be provided with housing and work until they become self-sufficient. If we don't want people to be forced back into crime, we must provide alternatives.

There will always be a few who choose to damage their cell, terminal, or other equipment. I believe very few will damage their only access to the outside world. Having all water sources controlled electronically and prevented from overflowing by sensors would leave little else that could cause severe or costly damage. The inmate should have to live with damage caused intentionally, and be required to repair it as a condition of release. All of this serves to communicate that actions have consequences, and may instill a sense of responsibility.

Prison inmates are people, and should be treated as such. If we want them to be rehabilitated, then we must provide a safe environment that is free of criminal influence, sex, drugs, alcohol, or even cigarettes. Inmates should receive proper nutrition and all their essential personal needs. If they choose to participate in religious services, they should be allowed to do so by terminal, providing no other inmate can be seen or heard. Most importantly, there must be no opportunity for criminal activity of any kind.

In a previous chapter, I told the story of my encounter with a violent juvenile offender and his gang. Why was he allowed to commit twenty-seven violent crimes before the age of seventeen? The young criminal can be the most dangerous of all, and should be treated as such. Age is not a factor, the willful commission of violent crime is. I don't believe we want them placed in the present prison system, which is little more than a university for crime. Reform schools and juvenile detention centers do little to rehabilitate them. We must always keep the protection of society foremost in our minds.

There may be people who think this cruel and unusual punishment. It's not punishment at all. The inmate's physical needs are met. He is not abused in any way. Some psychologists could speculate that social deprivation might cause the inmate psychological harm. I would ask them, "As compared to what — getting gang raped, forced into drugs or criminal activity, intimidated, injured or killed?" A criminal who has committed the acts that put him in jail is already psychologically harmed. I reject the notion that someone can be guilty of a crime against society yet be considered sane. Truly sane people do not murder, rape, rob, cheat, or otherwise abuse their fellow man.

The bail system may be partly responsible for the incarceration rate in this country. An offender who cannot afford bail often pleads guilty to some offense to avoid lengthy trial delays and the uncertainty of trial outcomes. Inability to pay bail may also contribute to offenders' running from police rather than surrendering. If one is presumed innocent unless proven guilty, bail should not be imposed unless the offender is accused of violent crime or poses a danger to society. Failure to appear for court dates should be treated as an admission of guilt and result in immediate detention.

Mental health care, drug treatment programs, and social reeducation centers would help to reduce the incarceration rate. Drug addiction should be treated as a disease, not a crime. **No one should profit from the imprisonment of people, so private prisons must be abolished**. Transitional services suggested in previous chapters would serve to rehabilitate convicts who had served their sentences. Maximum sentences could be significantly reduced in isolation prisons. Life sentences should be reserved for the most violent criminals.

Over the last few years there have been numerous incidents of police and civilian shootings of black men, many of them innocent of any wrongdoing. There may be an undercurrent of racism in police departments, but other factors may also be involved. Since the terrorist attacks of 9/11/2001, police departments have become highly militarized. Their training focuses on force projection rather than de-escalation. Some police departments have succeeded in reducing the rate of murder and other violent crimes, most notably New York City. They have somehow managed to embrace the multiethnic nature of their population, while others, like Chicago, continue to suffer nonstop violence. There is no guarantee that the policies that worked in New York will work in Chicago or any other jurisdiction, but they are a good place to start.

"Distrust everyone in whom the impulse to punish is powerful!"

Friedrich Nietzsche *(1844-1900) German-Swiss philosopher and writer.*

FREEDOM OF SPEECH

Freedom of speech has been used as an excuse for peddling pornography, smearing opponents in political races, revealing the most intimate secrets of celebrities, inciting riots, lying about others, telemarketing, and verbal abuse. The time has come to clearly define the purpose of this precious right. It allows us to state our opinion on matters of politics, religion, economics, or any matter of interest to us. It does not, in any way, obligate others to listen to us, nor does it obviate the right to privacy. This freedom should allow us to express anything we want, but not necessarily any way we want. Too many lives have been ruined by lies and innuendo.

Civilization is founded on truth. We believe that when we put our money in a bank, it will be there when we need it, and that it will accrue interest at the rate promised. When we give a contractor a down payment to cover the cost of materials for a remodeling job, we can believe he will complete the job. When we hand our credit card to a store clerk, we expect that our credit card bill will only show the items and amounts we charged. People testifying in court are required to tell the truth. We have a right to the truth in most matters.

In the 2000 presidential campaign primaries, George Bush was facing John McCain in South Carolina. McCain was leading. Voters in the state received phone calls asking whether they knew that McCain had a black daughter. The implication was that he had fathered her with a black woman. The truth was that he and his wife had adopted a Bangladeshi girl. Their act of kindness became McCain's undoing. The Bush campaign took advantage of the racial prejudice there. McCain's loss drove down polls in other states. Constant media coverage did the rest. Politics trumps charity.

In the 2004 election, John Kerry, a decorated veteran of the Vietnam War, who commanded a swiftboat on the rivers there, was accused of fabricating his exploits. One man he rescued and seven of his crew fully supported the official report that gave Kerry the medals. One crewmember did not. Kerry had turned against the war after serving in it. Somehow he was made to appear unpatriotic. He lost the election. Politics trumps truth.

In the 2008 presidential election, Donald Trump and other conspiracy theorists falsely asserted that Barack Obama was ineligible to be President of the United States because he was not a natural born citizen of the U.S. At least twenty-five percent of people, mostly Republicans, continued to

FREEDOM OF SPEECH

believe this lie for several years despite Obama's release of his birth certificate and subsequent confirmation by the state of Hawaii. Politics trumps truth. In my opinion, the perpetrators of these character assassinations should have been prosecuted, convicted, and imprisoned.

It should be apparent to anyone with an open mind that we have been conditioned to accept as fact concepts that cannot withstand close scrutiny when confronted with facts, figures, and historical evidence. In nearly every domain, some persons or entities have something to gain from promoting a particular viewpoint. Marketing and public relations firms, psychologists, political advisers and others have become expert at shaping our opinions. It becomes increasingly difficult to determine whether they are reflecting our opinions or we are reflecting theirs. In too many cases, their interests do not coincide with ours. Who are they? What do they have to gain? How do they affect us? These are all questions we must ask if we are to make choices that are in our own best interest.

The news media should report facts accurately, and not manufacture or sensationalize the news. They can certainly state their editorial opinions, or report the opinions of others, but facts should not intentionally be misstated, nor should others' statements be taken out of context. Tabloids have ruined people's lives by printing totally false stories about them. News media should be held to a higher standard. It is true that people can defend their reputations in the courts, but who can afford to do so? Freedom of speech should be the freedom to speak the truth or state an opinion without deriding others or inventing news.

There is a tendency in our society to value ourselves more highly than others. For example, we write the personal pronoun 'I' as a capital letter, but 'you' or anyone else is always lower case. We have lost the sense of 'us' being more important than 'I'. Winning has become the ultimate objective regardless of how the win is obtained. We taught our kids that how you win is more important than the win itself. When our younger son was twelve, he was enrolled in a Catholic school and played basketball. On several occasions, while playing against other Catholic schools, parents cheered when an opposing team's player got knocked to the floor by an intentional foul. This attitude has carried forward into political races where outrageous mudslinging has become the tactic of choice. The media suck it up because sensationalism sells. Real information about candidates is difficult to get. Investigative reporting costs money and news budgets are getting slashed. Is it any wonder that voter satisfaction with politicians is so low?

FREEDOM OF SPEECH

When we hire an executive in business, he or she must submit a resume of his or her experience and accomplishments. Misstatements usually lead to rejection. Should we not expect a resume of sworn accuracy from politicians? We should also expect a brief written statement of the candidate's position on key issues, and how he or she intends to deal with them. If the candidate has been in a legislative role before, a complete voting record, grouped by category, should be provided including a clear description of what the purpose of the bill was and the rationale for the vote. It should also disclose campaign contributions from any parties benefitting from the vote. In the case of judges, comparative statistics of convictions, sentences, and repeat offenses for various crimes, or awards for civil cases, would enable me to make a more informed decision.

I simply don't vote for those whose records or positions are unclear to me. After hundreds of fifteen or thirty second ads attacking each other's character, I am left with the impression that neither candidate has anything to say about his or her own qualifications and so must have none. I refuse to vote for any candidate of any party who engages in this type of campaigning. Among their rights should be the reasonable expectation that things said about them are true. They who speak about others should have the responsibility for ascertaining the truth of what they are saying or to categorize their statements as rumors or speculation. In my opinion, intentional lying to damage others should be a prosecutable crime. That in no way undermines anyone's right to free speech, the free expression of their opinions on any subject they choose.

There is no place in civilized society for verbal abuse, threats, intimidation, or humiliation of others. Profanity is also in no way necessary for communicating our ideas. All of these stand in the way of effective communication, and only serve to divide us.

I am a firm believer in the people. If given the truth, they can be depended upon to meet any national crisis. The great point is to bring them the real facts.

Abraham Lincoln

GOVERNMENT OF, BY, FOR PEOPLE

"We the People of the United States, **in Order to form a more perfect Union, establish Justice, insure domestic Tranquility, provide for the common defence, promote the general Welfare, and secure the Blessings of Liberty** to ourselves and our Posterity, do ordain and establish this Constitution for the United States of America."

When our founding fathers wrote "general Welfare" into the constitution, they did not mean that everyone should be on welfare. They meant "wellbeing" for all. That entire preamble defines the role of government. Government was supposed to be the friend and protector of the people. Even those who wrote those words were not perfect. They were slave owners and slaves were each considered to be only two-thirds person.

Over the last several decades, many candidates for political office have run to reduce the size of government, drain the swamp, reduce the role of government, etc. If government is so bad, why are they all fighting to get in? Maybe it isn't so bad for those in Congress and the White House. For many of us it has fallen far short of the ideals the founders set out for it. The notion that we should be able to do everything for ourselves is very faulty indeed. If we were able to do so, we would not need insurance companies.

Some issues are just too huge for individuals, insurance companies, and states to deal with. Among these are national defense, natural disasters, epidemics, international treaties, environmental protection, space exploration, as well as interstate and international commerce, transportation, and communications. The founders had little or no needs in many of these areas. We do. A small government cannot address them all. We don't need a small government. We need an efficient one that can address them all in a fiscally responsible way.

One administration wanted to increase voluntarism and charitable giving to deal with poverty and misfortune. They coined the phrase "a thousand points of light". I wanted to be one of those bright points. A couple (our friends) approached me wanting to borrow two thousand dollars to keep from losing their home. After much deliberation, I refused. I realized that they were so indebted that adding another loan would only make them more indebted and would only buy them one to two more months in their home. I agonized over it because I had seen firsthand how difficult it is for people to dig their way out of homelessness. I would have to take the money out of our IRA retirement savings. I offered to give them one of our cars and a few hundred dollars, as much as we

GOVERNMENT OF, BY, FOR PEOPLE 169

could afford. It didn't help. He owned a garbage truck that collected certain industrial waste materials. A change in environmental regulations raised his dumping fees up several hundred percent driving him out of business. His wife's diabetes went out of control and she died.

Individually there is little we can do to lift people out of poverty however they got there. We can throw them a life preserver, but we cannot lift them out of the water. The five dollars I give the beggar on the street corner only buys him one meal and enables him to return to that corner the next day.

Think of government as a giant insurance company, much like auto, home, business, and life insurance. We pay our premiums in taxes so we can be made whole if we are injured by others, but not if the injuries are self inflicted. The wealthy with their many possessions pay more even if they never suffer a loss. Those who do suffer a loss are protected from financial ruin and are therefore able to pay their insurance premiums (taxes) and support the businesses that keep the economy healthy.

Governments that do not understand this are soon overthrown either through revolt of its citizens or other nations which catch up to and surpass them economically and militarily. Just spending hundreds of billions of dollars on the next whizz-bang super military aircraft, missile, or ship (which they can knock off and produce for a fraction of that cost) will not forestall the inevitable. We must be strong militarily, but we are strongest when we have many friends and partners internally and internationally. A non-threatening posture must be maintained with potential enemies in order not to provoke them into building up their military capacity. The recent joint military exercises by Russia and China are clearly a reaction to our administration's aggressive posture. It is okay for a big man to have a big stick as long as it looks like a walking stick, he speaks softly and has a smile on his face.

"I hate war as only a soldier who has lived it can, only as one who has seen its brutality, its futility, its stupidity."

"The problem in defense is how far you can go without destroying from within what you are trying to defend from without."

"Every gun that is made, every warship launched, every rocket fired, signifies in the final sense a theft from those who hunger and are not fed, those who are cold and are not clothed."

Dwight D. Eisenhower (1890-1969), 34th President of the United States, Supreme Allied Commander Europe in World War II.

CONCLUSION

If after reading this book you still believe you are living in a capitalist democracy, then you must not understand what either term means. If you still believe either party's agenda is in the best interest of all the people, you are sadly mistaken.

We and many other nations are headed toward fascism. The rise of white supremacists and neo-Nazis and overconcentration on the military and business interests are symptoms. Let's not fall prey to the disease. Some call it nationalism or populism when, in fact, it has little to do with the people.

Not every aspect of our lives must provide an opportunity for financiers to profit at our expense. Every resource we exploit or deplete today deprives our children and their children of it in perpetuity.

We keep voting the same crowd back into Congress, yet hardly anyone is satisfied with the job they are doing. They came in with a promise of small government. What we got was one devoid of accomplishments. Every bill that has been pushed through by one party in the last few decades contains poison pills included by the other party. Any compromise between two bad options is certain to please no one.

It is time to restore confidence in our government. They must earn our trust or we must replace them with those who will obey the will of the people. If we want ideal results, we must first let go of failed ideologies and recognize that there are potential solutions that are good for everyone — the general wellbeing the Constitution promises.

The program I have laid out in this book can restore fairness and social and fiscal responsibility in business and government. But, it can only do so if you force Congress to enact the proposed reforms.

It is time to **Rise Up, people!**

Author Biography

E. J. (Gene) Schwarz was born under Soviet occupation of Eastern Poland during World War II. His family survived two Nazi concentration camps, where an injury combined with starvation disabled him. He only regained the ability to walk near the end of the war. Not wanting to return to communist controlled Poland, the family was placed in a refugee camp in Wildflecken, Germany. Four years later, they immigrated to the United States sponsored by a small church in Perry County, Arkansas, then the poorest in the U.S. Moving to Chicago in 1952, his parents found factory jobs and Gene continued his education. He attended Holy Trinity High School, became a self-taught industrial engineer and was employed by two management consulting firms, later starting his own firm. Having lived the American Dream as a U.S. citizen, he is now retired from senior management in international business. He has devoted more than forty years to the study of the Bible and History. He and his wife reside in Colorado Springs, Colorado, where he conducts seminars and writes on religion and socio-economic issues. He earned Advanced Catechetical Certification from the Roman Catholic Diocese of Colorado Springs.

Wildflecken Refugee Camp 1946, Prayers in makeshift church.

Aboard the General Altingen 1949, arriving in New Orleans

AUTHOR BIOGRAPHY 175

Home in Perry County, Arkansas, $5/month rent

Mother feeding chickens, 1951

Chicago 1953, Receiving religious award

EIGHT BOY SCOUTS of St. Hedwig parish, 2226 N. Hoyne, smiled as they were presented Ad Altare Dei awards on June 19. Rev. Felix S. Miliskiewicz, C.R., scout chaplain made the presentation to members of troop 28. Scouts (left to right) are: William Stefaniuk, Richard Krajewski, Ronald Lebowski, Leonard Dojnik, Thomas Ciszewski, Eugene Schwarz, Edwin Adeszko

Gene Schwarz named executive VP at Selfix

CHICAGO—Gene Schwarz has been named executive vice president and chief administrative officer for Selfix Inc.

Schwarz is responsible for all internal operations at the company.

Before assuming his new post, Schwarz was vice president/manufacturing and engineering for Selfix. He has been with the company for 13 years.

Housewares 11/5/1984

Selfix, Inc., 4501 W. 47th St., Chicago, IL 60632
Selfix of Canada, Ltd., Scarborough, Ontrario M1H 2V5
Selfix (Housewares) Ltd., Milton Keynes, MK1 1NN England
Selfix GmbH, D-6082 Mörfelden, West Germany